The
Guinea Pig
HANDBOOK

SHARON L. VANDERLIP, D.V.M.

BARRON'S

Acknowledgments

Thank you to my husband, Jack Vanderlip, D.V.M., for his invaluable help as an expert consultant in laboratory and exotic animal medicine. His supportive behind-the-scenes activities included obtaining scientific resources and critically reviewing the final manuscript and taking a genuine interest in my work.

A Note on Pronouns

Many guinea pig lovers feel that the pronoun "it" is not appropriate when referring to a beloved pet. For this reason, guinea pigs are referred to as "he" or "she" throughout this book.

About the Author

Sharon Vanderlip, D.V.M., has provided veterinary care to exotic and domestic animal species for more than 35 years. She has written books and articles in scientific and lay publications. Dr. Vanderlip served as the Associate Director of Veterinary Services for the University of California at San Diego School of Medicine, has worked on collaborative projects with the Zoological Society of San Diego, is former Chief of Veterinary Services for the National Aeronautics and Space Administration (NASA), is a consultant for universities, and has her own veterinary practice. She has received various awards for her writing and dedication to animal health.

Dr. Vanderlip was first introduced to guinea pigs as a child, when she owned and raised cavies as a hobby. Her fondness for these gentle, affectionate animals persists, and she is dedicated to providing them quality health care.

Cover Photos

Shutterstock: Danny Xu: front cover; Miroslav Hlavko: inside front cover, spine; photos2013: back cover (top); RamonaS: inside back cover; vovan: back cover (bottom)

Photo Credits

Shutterstock: ADA_photo: page 141; Ase: page 155; eAlisa: pages 6, 66, 128, 134, 135, 144; Birute Vijeikiene: page 19; Colette3: page 39; cynoclub: page 15; Elya Vatel: pages 42, 80; Eric Isselee: pages 5, 20, 21, 43, 75, 77, 81, 85, 92, 97, 150; E. Spek: page 11; Gordana Sermek: pages 41, 71, 78, 157; Graffiti Guild: page 4; gurinaleksandr: pages 28, 156; Jiri Krajicek: pages 28, 153; Jiri Pavlik: page 47; joannawnuk: pages 52, 88, 112, 136, 138; jordache: page 154; kerstiny: pages 37, 44; La India Piaroa: page 100; Kizel Cotiw-an: page 87; KPG Payless2: page 110; Kreangkrai Indarodom: page 46; Kristo-Gothard Hunor: pages 69, 152; Kuttelvaserova Stuchelova: page vi; melis: page 109; Miroslav Hlavko: pages 16, 27, 81, 113, 114, 121; Nastya Glazneva: page 158; Nathan clifford: pages 50, 105; Nicky Rhodes: page 24; Nikol Mansfeld: page 30; NotarYES: pages 30, 32; Onishchenko Natalya: page 147; Oshchepkov Dmitry: pages 90, 140; Petr Pajpach: page 110; PHOTO FUN: pages 12, 40, 84, 98, 103, 115; Photok.dk: page 142; PhotoSky: page 151; photos2013: pages 54, 95, 107, 117, 161; Ralph Loesche: pages 2, 72; RedTC: page 14; Rene Sputh: page 118; Rossignolek: pages 145, 146; Sascha Preussner: page 60; Studio DMM Photography, Designs & Art: page 9; Tim Large: page 18; TJ Images: page 65; Valeri Potapova: page 149; Vasily Kovalev: page 63; Vera Zinkova: page 130; VikaRayu: pages 13, 53; Vitaly Titov & Maria Sidelnikova: page 76; xstockerx: pages 26, 56, 82; Zadiraka Evgenii: page 139

All inquiries should be addressed to:
Barron's Educational Series, Inc.
250 Wireless Boulevard
Hauppauge, New York 11788
www.barronseduc.com

ISBN: 978-1-4380-0509-6

Library of Congress Catalog Control No. 2015938471

Printed in China
9 8 7 6 5 4 3 2 1

3361405649 2456

Contents

Chapter One
What Is a Guinea Pig?

Ask anyone what a guinea pig is and you'll be sure to hear all kinds of vivid descriptions of a bright-eyed cuddly creature that makes an excellent pet. But just what *is* a guinea pig? You have to admit, this curious name conjures up all kinds of images!

The Name Game

Guinea pigs are domesticated, tailless rodents native to the west coast of South America. Their wild cousins can still be found in Argentina, Uruguay, and Brazil. So, obviously, guinea pigs did not originate in Guinea and they are not pigs. They are not even relatives of the pig family! Yet the name "guinea pig" has persisted in several languages for hundreds of years. And that's not the only misnomer guinea pigs have been assigned. They have been called everything from *meerschweinchen* (German for little sea pig), to *lapin de Barbarie* (French for Barbary rabbit), to *porchita da India* (Portuguese for little pig from India—the reference to India might be because South America was considered part of the Indies by early navigators).

To learn how the guinea pig received its many nicknames and became a popular pet throughout the world, we need to slip back into the past and review the little bit we *do* know about this gentle animal's mysterious history.

Mysterious Ancestry

A native of South America, guinea pigs were domesticated thousands of years ago. Although there has been scientific disagreement about which species is the direct ancestor of today's guinea pig, crossbreeding and biochemical studies indicate that today's pet guinea pig probably descended from either the wild species *Cavia aperea* (found in Brazil, Ecuador, Paraguay, Uruguay, and northern Argentina), or *Cavia tschudii* (found in Peru, Bolivia, northern Chile, and northwestern Argentina), or *Cavia fulgida* (from southeastern Brazil). Charles Darwin, the famous naturalist and explorer, did not agree that *Cavia aperea* could be the ancestor of the guinea pig (*Cavia porcellus*), because the domestic guinea pig and *Cavia aperea* each had their own genus of parasitic louse.

No matter which wild species is the true forebear of our modern-day guinea pig, we now know that guinea pigs are distinct from each of the wild species. In fact, shortly after their introduction into Europe, guinea pigs became extinct in the wild.

From Kitchens to Continents

In ancient times, the Incas kept guinea pigs for food and offered them as sacrifices to their gods. The Andean Indians allowed guinea pigs to run loose in their kitchens. These South American Indians kept guinea pigs for food and as pets, selectively breeding them for variations in coat color, patterns, and textures, as well as flavor subtleties.

In November 1532, the course of guinea pig history was changed forever when the Spanish conquistador, Francisco Pizarro, and his small group of Spanish soldiers invaded the Incan Empire and captured the Incan Emperor "sun god" Atahuallpa. Pizarro and his men killed 80,000 Incan soldiers and eventually killed Atahuallpa as well. At the time of the Peruvian conquest, guinea pigs had already been domesticated and used as a food source for at least 3,000 years in their native land. It is reported that guinea pigs were frequently offered as sacrifices to the "sun god." Amidst the invasion and the battles, the gentle, mild-mannered, and peaceful guinea pig was "discovered." With the conquest of the Incan Empire, guinea pigs found their way from the Incan kitchens and sacrificial altars to the dining tables of the Spanish Colonial Empire, where they were sometimes referred to as *conejo*, or rabbit. But far more important, from that point on, guinea pigs also became world travelers and, in their own way, made their indelible mark on the world and in history.

Being small, guinea pigs were easy to transport, and in the sixteenth century Dutch sailors introduced the animals to Europe, where they were referred to as "guinea pigs." It has been speculated that roasted guinea pigs in the marketplace reminded the Europeans of suckling pigs and that's how they got their name. Some people think guinea pigs derived their name from the squealing sounds they make, similar to a pig's squeal (fortunately, not nearly as loud). Others suggested that "guinea" was synonymous with "foreign" in early days. Some researchers speculate that the guinea pig may have come to Europe on ships that departed from Guiana, in northeastern South America, or via slave ships departing from Guinea in West Africa, and so received the name "guinea." The truth is, we just don't know exactly how this unique creature acquired its bizarre name.

Introduction to the United States and Europe

Upon its arrival in Europe, more than 450 years ago, the guinea pig was a big success. Its affectionate, charming character and gentle nature quickly earned it a place as a beloved household pet. Its popularity spread rapidly throughout Europe where geneticists and hobbyists alike were smitten by its variety of coat colors, patterns, textures, and lengths. Guinea pig fanciers soon united and began raising the animals as a hobby for fun and entertainment. They traded animals and information and kept records on the various coat colors and types produced through selective breeding.

C. porcellus (Chile and Venezuela)
C. aperea (Brazil, Ecuador, Paraguay, Uruguay, and northern Argentina)
C. tschudii (Peru, Bolivia, northern Chile, northwestern Argentina)
C. fulgida (southeastern Brazil)

The guinea pig's portable size and social personality made it an ideal pet. It didn't take long for the good news to spread. As early as the seventeenth century, guinea pigs were exported to North America, where

they became popular companion animals for children and adults.

Since the mid-1800s, laboratories around the world have used guinea pigs as research models to study nutrition, genetics, toxicology, and pathology. It is a well-known fact that in this capacity guinea pigs have done more than their fair share to contribute to medical science and to the health and well-being of humans and animals worldwide. Today, guinea pigs are used much less in laboratories than in earlier times, especially when compared to other rodent species.

Guinea pigs are still raised in captivity and used as a source of food in Ecuador, Peru, and Bolivia. Fortunately for guinea pigs in Europe and North America, they are appreciated for their entertaining personalities and excellent companionship and not for their flavor. They now hold a

well-deserved place in our hearts as lovable pets—and this is where they will definitely remain!

The Guinea Pig Is a Cavy

If the guinea pig's common name is an inaccurate description at best, we can naturally ask if there isn't a better name for our endearing pets. The answer is a resounding yes! Although guinea pigs are still referred to as "guinea pigs" by scientists in research laboratories, it is ironically the guinea pig owners, breeders, and fanciers who call their pets by their correct name, "cavy" (pronounced "kay-vee"). Cavy comes from the species' scientific name, *Cavia porcellus*—a name that combines the cavy's evolutionary ancestry with the misconceptions of the early navigators.

As you read about cavies in magazine articles and books in the popular press, you may find them incorrectly referred to as *Cavia aperea*. Today's domestic guinea pig is a separate and distinct species from *Cavia aperea* and the other six species of cavies in existence. *Cavia aperea*, *Cavia fulgida*, or *Cavia tschudii* may be distant ancestors of our modern-day cavy, but there is still lively discourse in the scientific community about which one of these species can take the credit. In any case, our beloved *Cavia porcellus* is an independent entity that does not exist in the wild.

No matter what the evolutionary ancestry or domestication history, it seems the cavy will never quite shake itself free of earlier misnomers—even with its "modern scientific name"—for *porcellus* is Latin for "little pig!"

A Special Kind of Rodent

This pet belongs to a group of the most successful, diverse, and numerous of mammalian species: rodents. The words rodent and rodentia are derived from the Latin word *Rodere*, which means "to gnaw." This refers to a rodent's need to constantly chew on hard objects to keep the teeth from growing too long. The most important characteristic shared by all rodents is the continual growth of their front teeth throughout their entire lives. To better understand your cavy's personality, habits, instincts, and various requirements, it helps to have an appreciation of what a rodent is.

Rodents are remarkably uniform in structural characteristics and are grouped and classified according to anatomical characteristics, similarities in teeth and bone structure, origin, and lifestyle. All rodents have four incisors—two upper and two lower (the lower incisors are longer than the upper incisors). These front teeth grow throughout life, continuously being pushed up from the bottom of the jaw. This growth compensates for the constant wear on the teeth from biting hard objects and abrasion between the upper and

Pearly Whites

Most rodents have yellowish orange teeth, but cavies normally have white incisors.

lower pairs that maintain a chisel-like sharpness.

There are no nerves in the front teeth, except at the base where they grow, and continual wear of the incisors maintains very sharp cutting surfaces. Rodents do not have canine teeth or anterior premolars, so there is a rather large space, called the *diastema,* between the front teeth and the cheek teeth (premolars and molars). Like the incisors, a cavy's cheek teeth grow continuously throughout its lifetime. They are used for grinding (cavies grind and gnaw; they do not chew) and may have many peculiar patterns. These dental patterns, as well as jaw structure, are useful to zoologists and paleontologists for deter-

Dental Formula for the Adult Cavy

i 1/1, c 0/0, p 1/1, m 3/3 = 20

The number to the left of the slash represents one-half of the upper jaw (left or right side) and the number to the right of the slash represents one-half of the bottom jaw (left or right side).

i = incisors
c = canine teeth
p = premolars
m = molars

For example, there is one incisor in the upper jaw on the right side and one incisor in the right side of the lower jaw, no canine teeth in the mouth, one premolar in the right side of the upper jaw, and one premolar in the right side of the lower jaw. Finally, there are three molars in the right side of the upper jaw and three opposing molars in the right side of the lower jaw for a total of ten teeth. Multiply ten by two, to include all the teeth on the left side of the mouth, and the total number of teeth equals twenty.

mining how different rodent species developed over time, their relationship to each other, and their origin.

You are, no doubt, already familiar with some more common rodents, such as rats, mice, and hamsters, but cavies not only *look* different,

Cavy Classification

Animals, insects, and plants are classified and grouped according to their differences and similarities. Names are assigned according to kingdom, phylum, class, order, family, genus, and species. With each progressive category, animals grouped together are more closely related. For example, all animals are part of the Kingdom Animalia, but only rodents are members of the Order Rodentia.

Animals can be named according to a special characteristic of their group, named after the person who discovered them, or even named after the geographical area they naturally inhabit.

they *are* different. For example, they have special nutritional requirements, unique drug sensitivities, and specific behaviors. They have a much longer gestation period (two months compared to three weeks) and give birth to precocious offspring (rats, mice, and hamsters give birth to naked, helpless young whose eyes don't open for 10 to 14 days). Your pet is no "ordinary rodent!"

The Cavy's Place in Natural History

The cavy is a member of the King-dom Animalia (Animal Kingdom), the

Species Name	Country of Origin
Cavia porcellus	Chile and Venezuela The domestic cavy is now found worldwide, but no longer exists in the wild
Cavia anolaimae	Bogota vicinity, Colombia
Cavia aperea	Argentina, Brazil, Ecuador, Paraguay, Suriname, Uruguay
Cavia fulgida	Brazil
Cavia guianae	Brazil (possibly), Guyana, Venezuela
Cavia magna	Brazil, Uruguay
Cavia nana	Bolivia
Cavia tschudii	Argentina, Bolivia, Chile, Peru

Phylum Chordata (animals having spinal columns), and the Class Mammalia. The word "mammalia" refers to the mammary glands (mammae, teats, or breasts). Newborn and baby mammals are nourished by milk from their mothers' breasts. All warm-blooded animals with hair or fur have mammary glands and belong to the Class Mammalia.

Within the Order Rodentia, there are three suborders. The cavy belongs to the Suborder Caviomorpha. Caviomorph rodents are believed to be descendants of African Phiomorpha, a group of animals that lived during the Oligocene Period approximately 40 million years ago.

The Caviomorpha suborder is made up of 29 Recent rodent families. In paleozoological terms, the word "Recent" refers to the Recent Era, which corresponds to the end of the last ice age, about 13,000 years ago. The cavy belongs to the Superfamily Cavioidae and the Caviidae family. It has been suggested that the word "Cavia" comes from the Latin

Cavy Terminology
- Male cavies are called boars.
- Female cavies are called sows.
- Baby cavies are called pups.
- When a sow gives birth to her pups, it's called "farrowing."
- A group of cavies is called a herd.

word for cave, but some natural historians believe the word Cavia is possibly derived from the Indian name Coüy or from Cabiai, named by tribes in French Guiana. According to the fossil record, Caviidae first appeared in South America in the Late Miocene period (26 to 7 million years ago).

Families may be further divided into genera (plural for genus), a collection of even more closely related animals. There are 426 rodent genera. There are five Recent genera and 17 species in the Caviidae family.

The *Cavia* genus includes eight species, including the cavy, or guinea pig, whose scientific species name is *porcellus*.

Cavy Taxonomy
Kingdom Animalia
Phylum Chordata
Class Mammalia
Order Rodentia
Suborder Caviomorpha
Superfamily Cavioidae
Family Caviidae
Genus *Cavia*
Species *porcellus*

Complicated Caviomorphs

Cavies are caviomorphs. Caviomorphs are tailless South American rodents that are characterized by having one pair of mammae (teats), four digits on the forefoot, and three digits on the hind foot, as well as special anatomical features of the head and jaws.

As you study more about cavies, you may come across literature that refers to them as South American hystricognaths or hystricomorph rodents. Don't let this confuse you. The word "hystricomorph" has both systematic classification and structural meanings. Hystricomorph refers to a particular type of skull and muscle structure seen in certain rodent species, and a very rare type of bottom jaw structure and angulation, called a *hystricognathous mandible.* These different zoological names simply reflect what scientists believe about the origins and evolution of the cavy and its ancestors through the ages.

The Controversial Cavy

Cavies are not only complicated, they're controversial. If you think the nomenclature, taxonomy, fossil record, and theories of evolutionary history are complicated, you're right. It has taken zoologists and paleontologists countless years of study and research to sort through the scant evidence natural history has provided. And there is not always total agreement among the experts.

In the 1990s, a group of scientists studied some genetic material from cavies, rats, and mice and compared them. These researchers suggested that the cavy and other South American rodents are different enough from rats and mice that they should be removed from the Order Rodentia. They believed that the cavy and its close relatives should be assigned an order of their own.

Additional research since then supports the vast majority of scientists who maintain that the cavy is definitely a rodent and must remain classified in the Order Rodentia. This group of scientists reminds us that many anatomical features are specific to rodents, such as the bone structure and musculature of their entire head region, the teeth, and jaw musculature. There are also additional features characteristic of rodents that are not evident on the surface. For example, the fetal membranes found in rodents are unique among mammals, as well as their pattern of fetal development. And all of these rodent traits are found in the cavy.

We have learned a lot about the cavy, but each new discovery makes us ask new questions. It seems the cavy is destined to be the "laboratory guinea pig" until we have extracted the very last of its secrets—and by the looks of things, these revelations won't be any time soon.

Yet, with all the uncertainty, this much is clear: We now have a greater appreciation for the history and mysteries surrounding our charming caviomorph companions. And no matter what name you use—cavy or guinea pig—this shy, gentle animal is arguably the most beloved, interesting, and attractive of the more than 2,000 species of rodents in existence today.

Cavy Characteristics

Appearance

Weighing only 3 ounces (85–100 g) at birth and gaining 1 to 2 pounds (700 to 1,100 g) by the time it is fully grown, a cavy requires both hands to hold it securely and comfortably. From the tip of its nose to the end of its rump, an adult measures 8 to 10 inches (20.3 to 25.4 cm) in length and has no tail.

The endearing appearance of the cavy is partly attributable to its broad head, bright eyes, and rounded, rose petal-shaped ears that give it an impish, yet gentle, expression. The earflaps are virtually naked and set on a rather large head. Long whiskers accentuate the cavy's broad face. The eyes are located on the sides of the head, instead of the front of the face, to allow a wider field of vision so it is easier to detect approaching predators.

Cavies have a stocky, robust, compact body set on four short, delicate legs. The hind feet have three

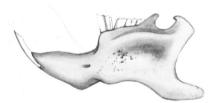

Lateral view (cheek side)

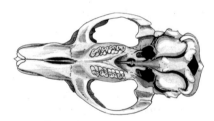

Ventral view (facing roof of mouth)

Medial view (tongue side)

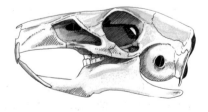

Side view

digits, and the front feet have four. All four feet have well-developed sharp claws. The footpads have no protective hair covering.

The hair, or pelage, consists of large guard hairs and an undercoat of fine hairs. The coat comes in a wide variety of colors and patterns and sheds easily. There are 13 cavy breeds and more than 20 color varieties recognized by the American Rabbit Breeders Association and the American Cavy Breeders Association. Depending on the breed, the coat may be smooth and short, or smooth and long, or coarse and short, or short and curly, or grow in long locks. In some breeds the hairs form whorls of tufts of hair in symmetric patterns called "rosettes."

Reproductive Characteristics

Compared to other rodents, the cavy has a relatively long gestation (pregnancy) period: 59 to 72 days.

(For example, hamsters have a gestation period of 16 to 18 days.) The length of cavy gestation is inversely proportional to the size of the litter. In other words, the larger the litter size, the shorter the gestation period. Also, the larger the litter size, the smaller the individual cavy pups are. The sow has only one pair of nipples located in the inguinal (groin) area, yet a healthy mother can nurse and raise several pups.

The sow has a bicornate uterus. That means that from the cervix, the uterus branches into a Y-shape, consisting of a left and a right uterine horn. This conformation enables the mother to carry offspring in each of the uterine horns.

Sows may begin their estrous cycles as early as four to five weeks of age (the average age is 67 days) and reach sexual maturity by ten weeks of age. Cavies are polyestrous (having more than one estrous cycle

Cavy Reproduction

Breeding Season	Year round
Estrous cycle	15 to 19 days
Duration of estrus	1 to 15 hours
Spontaneous ovulator	Yes
Implantation	7 days after fertilization takes place
Gestation	59 to 72 days (average 63 days)
Litter size	1 to 6 young (average 3)
Litters/year	3 to 5
Post-partum estrus	2 to 15 hours
Weaning	2 to 3 weeks of age
Sexual maturity (puberty)	Male: 3 to 4 months (550 to 700 g) Female: 2 to 3 months (350 to 450 g)

a season) and breed any time of the year. The estrous cycle lasts from 13 to 20 days, averaging 15 to 17 days. Cavies are spontaneous ovulators and estrus, the time period just before and just after ovulation, lasts 24 to 48 hours. Boars reach puberty (sexual maturity) at 56 to 70 days of age. For this reason, it is dangerous to leave very young sows in the presence of a boar. If they are bred too early in life, they will have difficulty carrying the pregnancy to term or have serious problems while trying to give birth and will die from complications. This information is important to have, because it means that it is possible for you to inadvertently acquire a cavy that is pregnant, even if she is very young, unless you can be sure that she was not housed with a boar at any time.

Most sows have a post-partum estrus, meaning they come back into estrus shortly after giving birth. The prolific cavy can lactate and feed a litter while maintaining a new pregnancy!

The male cavy reproductive system consists of the testes, epididymis, ductus deferens, urethra, vesicular glands, prostate, coagulating glands, and bulbourethral glands.

The testicles are retained in the open inguinal canal, and mature boars have large testes and obvious scrotal sacs. The penis is covered with small keratinized scales arranged in a pattern. Inside the penis is a small, flat bone (the os penis). There are two prongs of equal length at the tip of the penis.

Cavy pups are precocious, born fully haired with a full set of teeth,

Cavy Growth Guidelines

Age	Males	Females
Birth Weight Length	4 ounces (115 g) 3 inches (8 cm)	3 ounces (85 g) 3 inches (8 cm)
3 weeks (Weaning)	8.5 ounces (240 g)	6 ounces (165 g)
8 weeks	15 to 17 ounces (425 to 480 g)	13 to 16 ounces (370 to 450 g)
12 weeks	28 ounces (794 g)	22 ounces (624 g)
Adult Weight Length	33.5 to 42 ounces 2.1 to 2.6 pounds (950 to 1200 g) 10 inches (25.4 cm)	28 to 30 ounces 1.5 to 1.8 pounds (790 to 850 g) 8 inches (20.3 cm)

eyes wide open, and an ability to nibble on solid food. Although the babies can eat small amounts of solid food within a few days of birth, they still need their mother's milk until they are at least two weeks of age, preferably three weeks of age.

Senses

Cavies have a keen sense of smell. They also have very sensitive hearing, due to their large tympanic bullae and four cochlear coils. Studies have shown their hearing is sensitive in ranges of 500 to 8,000 Hz, and cavies can hear sounds ranging up to 50,000 Hz. This might explain why cavies are such good communicators. Their repertoire of vocalizations includes squeals, chirps, squeaks, whistles, churring sounds, and tooth chattering and grinding.

Research suggests that cavies may be able to detect the colors green and blue. A close look at specific cells of the eye, known as rods and cones, confirmed that cavies have two of the three types of cones necessary for color vision (dichromate). In addition, cavies can easily discriminate variations in brightness and object size.

Intelligence

Don't let your pet's big head fool you into thinking there's an equally large and impressive brain on the inside. Cavies are not known for their intelligence, as much as they are known for their charm! Cavies recognize their owners and return affection. They can adapt to habits and routines—*and* they know what it takes to make their owners cater to their every cavy desire. Just wait and see. Your pet will have you trained in no time. Before you know it, you'll be at your cavy's beck and call, feeding treats when it whistles and caressing him when he squeaks for affection. You'll be shopping for the perfect toys and trying to find a way to spend as much time as possible with your little companion. Cavies may not be brilliant, but they are definitely cuddly, comical, clever, and just a little bit conniving—so get ready to enjoy the cutest pet you'll ever know!

Chapter Two

Is a Cavy the Right Pet for You?

From the time of their discovery and domestication thousands of years ago in South America, cavies have made their way into the hearts and homes of people of all ages, all around the world. Cavies are loved for their gentle, affectionate nature and delightful personalities. Their attractive variations in coat colors and textures make them all the more appealing. It's no secret—cavies make wonderful pets for children and adults alike.

No wonder you are captivated by the charm of these shy, bright-eyed creatures with the soft expression. Who wouldn't want to bring one home? So let's take a closer look at cavies, so you will know if one (or more) is the right pet for you.

Not a "Pocket Pet"!

Cavies are sometimes referred to as "pocket pets," an affectionate, but outdated and inappropriate term for companion animals tiny enough to fit into your pocket. You would need a very large pocket to accommodate a cavy, especially an adult! A full-grown cavy can weigh 2 pounds (1 kg) or more. Besides, cavies are cuddlers. They prefer to sit on laps and be caressed, rather than be packed in a pocket.

Cavies are not demanding, but they do have special needs, including a comfortable loving home and a caring owner with plenty of time to snuggle.

Do Your Homework First

Just because cavies are small, doesn't mean there isn't a lot to consider before you can add one to your family. Responsible pet ownership always involves a certain amount of planning, commitment, time, and expense. In all fairness to yourself and your future pet, do your homework first and learn as much as possible about its special needs and behaviors. To know cavies is to love them. Learning all about them will not only help you decide whether a cavy is compatible with your lifestyle, but also which breed(s) is (are)

a good match for you and how many you can comfortably house.

Remember that cavies can live several years, so consider your long-range plans.

• Will you be changing jobs, going on vacation, starting college, moving, or adding a new baby or a new pet to the family?

• If you rent, does your landlord allow pets? (Some landlords may not allow cats and dogs, but will give permission for small pets if the tenant pays a modest deposit, so discuss these options with your landlord *before* you buy your pet.)

• Are you willing and able to feed, clean, and care for a pet for five or more years?

Take everything into consideration, both long- and short-term, so you don't end up in a dilemma where you can no longer keep your little companion and must give her up for adoption.

Note: Before you bring your cavy home, make sure you have everything prepared in advance for her arrival. A little bit of good planning will go a long way to ensure that things go smoothly for you and your new friend.

Are You a Good Candidate for a Cavy?

Cavies are delightful animals that are fun to watch and enjoy being held and petted. They are affectionate and easy to maintain in captivity.

But an *only* cavy is a *lonely* cavy. Because they are so sociable, it is best to house at least two animals together if you do not have a lot of time to share with your pet.

Here are some things to consider and help you decide if one or more of these gregarious critters would make a compatible companion for you.

1. Consider yourself and your family first. How you live and what you do are important factors in assessing how well a cavy will fit into your lifestyle. The addition of a new pet should be nothing less than a happy and positive experience.

2. It is well known that pet ownership has many benefits. For example, people who own animals have been known to derive certain physiological and psychological benefits from the close human-animal bond they form. Pet owners feel wanted, needed, and loved, and indeed they are. After all, their animals depend on them for food and care, and give affection and companionship in return. Caressing or holding an animal has even been shown to reduce blood pressure in some cases and medical research suggests that people who own pets may even live longer.

3. But owning a pet is not always easy. It is a long-term time commitment and financial responsibility. And along with the joys of pet ownership, there is the sadness that accompanies the eventual, and inevitable, illness, loss, or death of an animal friend. Naturally, the longer you have your cavy, the more attached to her you will be. Because they are so affectionate and can live so long, when they are gone they are dearly missed.

So, all things considered, are you a good candidate for a cavy? And are you ready and prepared to take on the responsibilities of owning and caring for this enchanting pet?

Can You Afford a Cavy?

Cavies are not expensive, although they are higher priced than more common, smaller rodent pets (rats, mice, hamsters, degus, gerbils). Some of the fancy breeds and varieties can bring a higher price than the more common varieties, especially if you are purchasing a very flashy animal for breeding purposes or exhibiting at the shows.

The purchase price of your pet will be minimal compared to the costs of housing, space, food, and veterinary care. Fortunately, quality cavy food is relatively inexpensive (although cavies are eager eaters), and so is the wide variety of toys you can buy or make for your pet.

Housing: Your biggest monetary expense will be housing, in the form of an indoor cage or pen, and bedding material. You should buy the most spacious and best-built cage and the best-quality bedding material you can afford. Housing and bedding are two areas where you should never scrimp when it comes to your pet's health and contentment.

Veterinary care: Cavies are relatively hardy pets, but it's always a good idea to have some money saved up in case your pet ever needs emergency veterinary care. By putting aside a small amount each month, veterinary care will be more affordable for you and the funds will be there when you need them.

There are also many companies that offer medical insurance for pets. Ask your veterinarian for a list of recommended pet insurance companies,

Time: The major investment you cannot truly measure is time. Set aside time to play with your cavy every day. This contact is important to keep your companion happy and well socialized. Cavies love to visit and snuggle with their owners. You must also take time to provide fresh food and water every day and clean the cage at least once a week. The amount of time and money you spend taking care of your little friend is small compared to the fun and affection she will give you in return. It is a wise investment to ensure that your bright-eyed companion is healthy and happy.

Other Household Pets

One of the biggest threats to a cavy's safety is the presence of another animal. Cavies have a very keen sense of smell. They know when there are other animals in the house and can become stressed or frightened if your other pets come near the cage. Make sure the lid or door to the cage is securely fastened. Be sure

to place the cage well out of reach of the family dog, cat, ferret, bird, or any other pet. You probably never thought of your house pets as being harmful, but cats and ferrets are natural hunters and dogs can play rough. Even birds can peck a rodent to death. And large pet reptiles just might find your cavy to be the ideal size for a meal, especially a baby cavy! Although cavies have been known to inflict bite wounds when frightened, they are not aggressive and seldom bite. Your small, mild-mannered pet is certainly no match for these animals.

Many people who keep cavies also keep other species of rodent pets. In fact, some report that cavies and other rodent species are compatible housed together in the same cage. Although it is tempting, *do not house your cavy with other rodents.* Most rodent pets are more likely to bite than cavies. They may seem to be getting along well right now, but when you leave the house you may return to find your cavy's ear par-

tially nibbled off, or a deep puncture wound on its back. Besides, cavies are often stressed by the presence of other rodents, so why upset them unnecessarily? More important, cavies are susceptible to many rodent diseases that can be carried by and shared with other rodent pets. Your other rodents may not appear ill, but they can spread infections to your cavy that can make her very sick.

Cavies are often housed with rabbits and almost always get along well with them, especially the smaller rabbit breeds, as long as there is enough space in the cage for everyone and lots of places to hide (hideaways and nest boxes). Unfortunately, just like rodents, healthy-appearing rabbits can spread serious diseases to cavies, such as *Bordetella* (see Chapter Eight, Cavy Health Care).

One of the more serious problems with housing other pet species and cavies together is that your cavy will naturally eat their food if it's available in the cage. And you *don't* want that to happen. Rabbit, mouse, and rat food are not good for cavies (see Chapter Five, Feeding Your Cavy). Cavies have special nutritional requirements that differ from those of other animal species.

For the safety of all the pets in your household, and in the best interests of your cavy's health, it is best to house your cavies separately from other species and keep them out of reach of other animals.

Can You Cavy-Proof Your Home?

Some of the more fun aspects of cavies—their small size, gentle temperament, and curious nature—also create some of the biggest problems for their safety. They can fit through

spaces you would never think possible. If your pet can squeeze its broad head through an opening, the rest of its rotund body will follow easily. And because they love to chew, you cannot keep cavies in wooden or cardboard containers as they will eventually gnaw and chew their way out.

Unlike many pets, cavies are not escape artists. In fact, they rarely try to escape from home at all. It's not unusual to find a cavy in its cage, chewing contentedly on some hay, hours after someone has forgotten to close the cage door! Cavies are not diggers (although they like to tunnel through shavings) and they are very poor climbers. They cannot cling, so they fall easily. They cannot jump well at all (although there have been reports of cavies jumping out of containers 12 to 18 inches [31 to 46 cm] high, but these are rare exceptions). It would seem that your cavy would never leave home, at least not intentionally.

Nevertheless, accidents happen. A child may forget to put your pet back in the cage after holding it, or a clever cat may work a latch open and startle your cavy from its safe haven. Whatever the circumstances, once your pet is loose in your home, she faces countless life-threatening situations, such as exposure to household chemicals, pesticides, rodent traps, electrical shock, bite wounds from other pets, and crushing injuries.

So before you let your cavy wander loose in the house, or before she accidentally escapes, make sure you take the time and trouble to make your house safe for your pet *before* you bring her home (see Chapter Six, Your Cavy Comes Home).

Always supervise your little companion when she is out of her cage and never let her wander out of your sight.

Are You Allergy Prone?

Allergies to animals are quite common; some people simply cannot have pets, no matter how much they love them. For example, people with allergies to pet dander or with compromised or suppressed immune systems cannot jeopardize their health by adding more allergens (pet dander, urine, or cage bedding and dust) to their environment.

No matter what breed of cavy you select, long hair, smooth hair, curly hair, or otherwise, it will shed sometime during the year. Even hairless cavies can cause allergies. Why? Because the allergen responsible for causing most allergies to rodents is urine. It is well documented that allergy-prone individuals can develop a specific sensitivity to rodent urine and dander; in fact, allergies to animals is an occupational hazard of veterinarians and laboratory workers.

Allergies usually develop over a long period of exposure. In other words, you may not be allergic to cavies right now because you may not have had a lot of exposure to them, but what about later? You certainly don't want to develop an allergy later on and have to part with your precious pet.

Check with your physician to determine if you are allergy prone. If your doctor gives you the go-ahead on owning a pet, first visit some cavy breeders, pet shops, or friends who own cavies. Try holding and petting one and linger a while. Go back and visit several times. If you develop any signs of an allergy—itchy and watery eyes, shortness of breath, rash, wheezing, coughing, or sneezing—then don't bring a cavy into your home. You risk harming your health and will eventually have to give your pet up for adoption.

On the other hand, if you don't have signs of allergies, there are some precautions you can take to reduce the chances of developing an allergy in the future.

• Don't keep your pet in the bedroom, where you would have close exposure to it for several hours each evening. There is no sense in unnecessarily exposing yourself to allergens while you are sleeping.

• Place your pet's cage in a well-ventilated, but not drafty, area of the house. If you have a small home, purchasing an air filter to keep the air fresh and free of dander and dust is a wise investment.

• Place absorbent paper underneath the bedding material. Absorbent paper is one of the best ways possible to lower exposure to allergy-causing substances, especially urine.

• Wear a mask and gloves when changing your pet's bedding. This might seem extreme, but it greatly reduces your chances of exposure to allergens. Gloves and a mask help prevent exposure through inhalation or contact. (If you are allergic to latex, buy vinyl gloves.)

• Take the cage outside to clean it. This prevents small particles from scattering throughout the house. In addition to urine, house mites (that can get into bedding) and wood shavings often cause allergies.

Children and Cavies

Cavies make wonderful pets for children. They are cute, calm, soft, and gentle. They are fun to hold and pet and enjoy sitting on laps. They are not likely to bite, although they do like to nibble on clothing and little fingers, so be careful!

Children naturally love small, warm, furry animals. They can't resist the temptation of rubbing a cheek against their pet's plush coat. And children love to show their affection by hugging and kissing their pets. As difficult as it may seem, for the health and safety of children in your

home, do your best to discourage this. Cavies are not biters, but keep in mind that the majority of all animal bite wounds inflicted on children (regardless of animal species) happen in the area of the face and head.

For the safety of your cavy, make sure children don't love your pet to death. Some children like to hug or squeeze pets just a little too enthusiastically. They don't realize how small and fragile an animal can be and they may accidentally squeeze too hard and injure your cavy. Teach

Ouch!
Never pick up a cavy by the nape of the neck, or by a limb, or by the ears.
• Improper handling can be painful.
• Your pet could be dropped and injured.

them that cuddling is fine, but they must be gentle.

Very young children must learn that it is safer for the animal if they observe it in its cage or hold it on their laps under direct adult supervision. Although your cavy may be calm around you and easy for you to handle, a stranger's voice, or a child's sudden movements, may startle it. If your pet is frightened, it may bite or squirm about and try to escape. It can easily slip out of a child's small hands in a heartbeat. Unfortunately, most cavies that are dropped are seriously injured. Even a fall from a short distance often results in a broken foot, leg, or back.

To prevent injury to your pet and heartbreak to the child, be sure to teach children in your home the correct way to pick up a cavy and how to hold it comfortably while supporting its body.

The safety of the child and your pet is your responsibility. When you cannot be there to supervise their activity, place the cage in a safe area and be sure the cage door is fastened securely. This is a safety measure well worth the temporary inconvenience.

The Magic Mediator

Some children are uncomfortable around animals, especially large ones. Children who have had a bad experience with animals in the past, such as having suffered a dog bite or a cat scratch, can greatly benefit from getting to know a calm, collected cavy. This small bundle of fuzz and tenderness can change a child's anxiety and fear into affection and interest. You can't ask for a better confidence builder.

With adult guidance, there is no limit to the things children can learn from a cavy. Cavy ownership provides an excellent opportunity for adults to teach children about pets, the importance of humane care and treatment, and respect for life. Young children can take part in the animal's daily care and learn about the importance of fresh water, good food, and a clean home. Caring for a cavy will help them develop a sense of responsibility.

Depending on their ages, children can learn about animal behavior, sleep patterns, exercise, nutrition, biology, reproduction, and even color genetics. In fact, older children can turn the knowledge they gain from their cavies into a school science project or a 4-H project. After all, some of these young cavy enthusiasts will become reputable, respected cavy breeders and exhibitors in the not too distant future and we'll need them to supply us with more of these adorable animals.

Cavies bring out the best in all of us by opening doors of communication. Even shy children will often talk freely when they are in the presence of animals. And somehow it's easier for adults to listen and respond—to children and to each other—while they are caressing a pet. Together families can share thoughts and ideas about animals and people and the importance of kindness and humane care. Holding and petting a cavy really does work magic within a family. Try it! You'll see why a cavy is the quintessential pet.

Chapter Three

Finding the Perfect Cavy

You have decided a cavy is the perfect pet for you. Great! Now it's time to find the perfect cavy—one that is the right match for you and your family. There are many types of cavies to choose from and lots of places to find them. So let's look at the options so you can be sure the cuddly character you select is happy and healthy. The main thing to keep in mind is that the health, personality, and age of your pet are more important than his color or hair type.

Where to Find a Cavy

Birds are found in aviaries. Bees are found in apiaries. Cavies are found in caviaries. Really! Cavy breeders and hobbyists call their cavy breeding facility a "caviary," just as dog breeders call their facilities "kennels."

Breeders: Fortunately, cavies are easy to find. The very best way to find a healthy, attractive, purebred cavy is to purchase from a reputable breeder.

For information on cavy breeders in your area, contact the Official American Cavy Breeders Association (ACBA). The ACBA is a charter of the American Rabbit Breeders Association (see Useful Addresses and Literature). The ACBA can give you the name, address, email address, and telephone number of the official cavy breeders association in your state, and the state association can then put you in contact with cavy fanciers near you.

ACBA breeders love their cavies and do their best to keep them healthy and happy and place them in the best homes. Breeders know their animals' genetics and family lines, ages, socialization conditions, and breeding and health records. And breeders usually have an excellent selection of fancy cavies available of various breeds and ages.

Pet shops: Pet shops almost always have cavies for sale, but they may not always have babies available. Pet stores usually sell mixed-breed cavies. These are animals that are a mixture of different cavy breeds, similar to a mixed-breed (or mongrel) dog. The fact that the

animal is a combination of breeds doesn't lessen its value as a precious pet. It just means that the animal is not a candidate for exhibition on the show table, where cavies must match up to specific high standards of appearance and conformation (called the "Standard of Perfection" by cavy show judges).

If you want a purebred cavy, you will have better luck contacting an ACBA breeder. Otherwise, you will have to make a special request in advance to the pet store and specify the breed, variety, gender, and age of animal you would like to purchase. It's not always possible to fill the order immediately, but if you are patient, the right cavy will come your way.

Internet ads: One of the easiest ways to find a cavy is to search for cavy breeders online and visit their websites. Start with the ACBA website. It is full of information!

Cavy Contacts
- American Cavy Breeders Association
- Local Cavy Breeders
- Pet Stores
- Veterinarians
- Internet websites
- Advertisements in Pet Magazines
- Animal Shelters
- Guinea Pig Rescue Groups

Veterinarians and owners: Your veterinarian may also know some cavy breeders you can contact. Finally, if you know people who own cavies, ask them where the animals were purchased. Word of mouth is often the best referral and testimonial.

No matter where you live, there is bound to be a cavy within driving distance of your home, just waiting for you to find it.

Assessing Cavy Conditions

You will have a lot of questions for breeders as you search for your perfect companion. The breeders will have plenty of questions for you, too, because they truly care about their cavies' future and well being. Their top priority should be placing their cavies with the right person, in an ideal home environment.

The kind of living environment a breeder provides animals gives you a lot of information about the care the animal receives. Whenever possible, once you have located a breeder, ask for an appointment to meet the breeder and to see the available cavies. If you are lucky, you might be able to see your future pets' parents, as well.

When you arrive at the breeder's, take note of the animals' home environment, including cleanliness, housing, and play areas. Areas should smell fresh and clean. Cages, housing, dishes, and toys should be clean. Observe the cavies closely. Are they healthy, happy, and alert?

If the housing conditions appear less than ideal, or if the animals appear unhealthy in any way, then continue your search for your perfect pet somewhere else.

Here are some questions you may want to ask the breeder:

1. How long has the breeder been raising cavies?

2. Is the breeder a member in good standing with the American Cavy Breeders Association?

3. What are the details of the breeder's health guarantee? Does the breeder provide a 48 to 72 hour health guarantee to give you time to have the cavy examined and declared healthy by your veterinarian?

4. Will the breeder help you find the cavy a home, if something unexpected happens to you that makes it impossible for you to take care of it?

5. What additional information does the breeder think is important for you to know about the cavy you have selected?

6. Can you contact the breeder in the future if you have additional questions?

Cavy Rescue

Sometimes you can find a suitable cavy at the local animal shelter or with the help of a rescue group (these groups are usually called Guinea Pig Rescue). These poor critters are in the shelter through no fault of their own. They may be well mannered and good natured, but because their owners could no longer keep them

Guinea Pig Rescue and Animal Shelters—
10 Questions for the Adoption Counselors

1. Why was the cavy given up for adoption?
2. Does it have a health problem?
3. Does it have a behavioral problem?
4. How old is it?
5. What sex is it?
6. Is it neutered?
7. Is it used to being housed singly or with other animals?
8. What type of food has it been eating?
9. What type of housing is it used to?
10. Does the animal have any special requirements?

and didn't take the time to personally find them a new home, they have been abandoned or relinquished to the shelter. Usually, cavies are given up for adoption because their owners moved, or the landlord did not allow pets, or there was a change in the family situation; or the owner could not afford veterinary care. Less frequently, allergy is the culprit.

All relinquished cavies have one thing in common: They desperately need, and would appreciate, a loving home. Before you adopt a cavy at the animal shelter, be sure to talk to the adoption counselor and learn as much as you can about him to be sure it is the right match for you. Cavies are set in their ways and there are some definite challenges

to adopting an adult. For example, cavies have difficulty adapting to changes in environment, housing, and food. And a cavy that hasn't been held daily will need some reassurance and an extra amount of socialization.

If you think a relinquished adult cavy could make a good companion for you, visit your local animal shelter. Take along a list of all of your questions to ask the adoption counselors.

The counselors can give you detailed information on each animal in their care. Be prepared to answer some questions about yourself as well. The adoption counselors will want to be sure their charismatic cavy is going to the perfect person and that it will never have to change homes and families ever again.

How to Choose Your Cavy

There are few things as adorable as a baby cavy pup. Unless you are planning on raising cavies and want to purchase adults from the onset, a pup is the way to go. It will quickly adapt to your home life and you will have most of its lifetime to enjoy it. Pups are easy to pick out in a group because they are smaller and more active than the adults. And let's be honest—they're much cuter, too!

• The best way to find a good-natured, healthy, attractive pup is to visit as many places as possible.

Cavies are very well developed at birth and their eyes are wide open. They are weaned at 21 days of age, when they weigh between 5.8 to 8.4 ounces (165 to 240 g).

• Try to find a weanling pup that is not much more than four weeks of age. Sows can reach sexual maturity as early as four to five weeks of age! Keep this in mind during your search. If you purchase a sow that is one month of age or older that has been housed with a boar, even for a brief period of time, chances are very good that she is pregnant, so be prepared for this possibility.

• Don't be an impulse buyer! It's a sure thing that the first (and second and third) cavy you see will tug at your heartstrings and you will want to buy it. But resist the temptation until you can visit as many breeders and pet stores as possible. Look at as many animals as you can *before* you make a selection. This way you can compare the overall health and quality of the animals, the cleanliness of their environments, their sociability, the different breeds, and the different price ranges.

• Never buy a pet because you "feel sorry for it." Animals that draw our sympathy—animals that are undersized, thin, scraggly, or isolated and withdrawn from the group—are the ones that are unwell and may cause you heartache later on. It's human nature to want to reach out to these unfortunate creatures and help them. You can't help but imagine how much better they would be in your cozy home under your personal care. But focus on your goal: Find a bright-eyed, healthy companion with a bubbly personality. Unless you are prepared for the time commitment, probable veterinary expenses, and disappointments that may accompany a sick or hapless animal, look for the healthiest, most outgoing, and inquisitive cavy you can find.

Hold Off on Holidays

Animals are often purchased during the holidays as gifts for someone else. This brings up three very important points.

1. Although it is tempting, it is never a good idea to buy a pet as a gift. Pet ownership is a responsibility that someone else may not want to assume.

2. Adding a new pet to the family during the holiday season should be discouraged. This is a time when most people already have plenty to do with visitors, deadlines, and commitments. A new pet can be overlooked in the busy shuffle with all the distractions and excitement. Families do not have time to learn about, observe, socialize, and care for a new pet during the holidays. Visitors and guests unfamiliar with proper handling techniques may stress and frighten the new arrival or drop it. Someone may forget to close the cage door or

lid. Holidays are a time when many pets escape from home or are lost.

3. Pets bought during the holidays may be more stressed or prone to illness than usual. With the greater demand for pets during this time, animals may be separated from their mothers and weaned too early, or shipped long distances in cold weather. These stressful situations can lead to illness and even death. There are, of course, animal protection laws, but it is good to be aware of potential problems.

Signs of a Sick Cavy

A sick cavy is quiet, listless, and dull. He may sit hunched up in a corner, away from all the activity, avoiding people and its fellow cagemates. Hair loss, weight loss, and loss of interest in its surroundings are signs

Isolation

If you already have cavies at home and the new cavy you have selected is an addition to the group, remember to keep the new cavy isolated from the others for at least one week to make sure it is not incubating a contagious disease. This will prevent accidental spread of disease to your other pets in case your new cavy develops an unexpected, contagious health problem.

of a sick cavy. Panting, sneezing, wheezing, coughing, discharge (from the eyes, ears, nose, mouth, or anus), diarrhea, and convulsing are all signs of a sick animal.

Warning: Never buy a cavy that was housed in a cage where another cavy showed signs of illness. The sick cavy may have a contagious disease and the other cavies in its cage could be incubating the disease and become ill several days later. If you buy a cavy that was housed with a sick cavy, he could fall ill a few days after you bring him home.

Signs of a Healthy Cavy

A healthy cavy is bright eyed and alert and interested in its surroundings—and he's interested in *you*. When you approach, he should sniff the air, advance cautiously to investigate, and, if you are very lucky, he may chirp, whistle, rumble, or squeak a happy greeting. This is a good sign! It means this is a cavy that is used to people and enjoys human company. And most likely this little critter is used to receiving hand-fed treats and expects a handout along with your visit.

Healthy cavies eat and drink a lot. They are active and inquisitive. In fact, they are usually not still for more than six to ten minutes at a time and average more than 20

Cavy Health Check
- Are the eyes bright and clear?
- Is the coat shiny?
- Is the skin healthy and free of parasites?
- Is the animal behaving normally?
- Does the cavy move and sit normally?
- Is it the right weight (not too thin and not too fat)?
- Check under the tail for signs of diarrhea.
- Check the mouth, eyes, ears, nose, anus, and genital area for signs of discharge.
- Are the teeth (incisors) properly aligned?
- Check for sores on the feet.
- Check for overgrown toenails.
- Is the animal pregnant?

hours of activity each day. No wonder they eat so much!

Once you have chosen a healthy cavy to take home, ask if you can pick him up and hold him before you buy him. You will quickly learn how much handling the animal has had and how mild mannered he is by how he behaves when you hold him. If he squeaks, squeals, squirms, and wiggles to free himself, hold him firmly but gently against your chest and speak to him softly and reassuringly. Give the small creature a little bit of time to calm down and get used to you. He should relax and enjoy your company and caresses after a few minutes. On the other hand, if the animal acts aggressively or tries to bite, this is not typical, cuddly cavy behavior. Continue your search for a more socialized, tame individual.

If the cavy you have selected is calm and allows you to hold him gently, examine him closely to be sure he is in good health.

• The eyes should be bright and clear.

• Ears should be clean and skin and hair should look healthy.

• Light shedding is normal at some times of the year, but bald patches and poor coat condition may mean the animal is sick or old.

• Examine the belly and the bottom of the feet to be sure there are no sores on them.

• Check the nails to be sure they are not overgrown or crooked and do not grow in odd directions.

• Make sure the animal sits and walks in a normal manner, and take time to observe that he is eating and drinking.

• It is especially important to examine the front teeth to check that they are properly aligned in the mouth. Dental misalignment causes many health problems and is usually an inherited problem. Animals with crooked, misdirected teeth should never be used for breeding.

The cavy you finally select will depend on availability, physical qualities, and your personal preferences. Of all the animals you have visited, which ones appeal the most to you?

Which are the most friendly, healthy, curious, and playful? Which ones have the best personality? Which ones enjoy snuggling close to you or sitting in your lap? Which ones are the most attractive and irresistible? The hardest thing about choosing a cavy to join your family is leaving the other ones behind.

How Many Cavies Should You Keep?

How many cavies you keep is purely up to you. Cavies should be fun. You never want to have so many animals that it seems you spend more time cleaning up after them than enjoying them. Your available free time and space will determine how many animals you can reasonably keep. To be on the safe side, start conservatively with just one or two animals. Later on, if you have enough time, space, knowledge, funds, and enthusiasm, you may eventually want an entire herd.

A single cavy can be great company and provide hours of entertainment. Cavies become very attached to their owners and love human interaction. If you can spend lots of time caressing and holding and playing with your pet, he will be perfectly happy and not miss being with other cavies. However, in all fairness to your pet, remember that cavies are very social animals that can become lonely. They are communal animals

that normally live in family groups and thrive on interactions with members of their own species. When they are not cuddling with you, they enjoy snuggling with each other. For these reasons, if your schedule requires long or frequent absences, it is highly recommended that you keep a minimum of two cavies to prevent loneliness and boredom.

Cavies thrive in small social groups of three to five. They also breed year round and are quite prolific. The best way to avoid unwanted cavy pregnancies is to house compatible females together, *without* a boar. On the other hand, if you have a preference for male cavies, bear in mind that they can be territorial and fight with each other, especially if they are housed with one or more females. If you decide to house boars together, make sure they are compatible and have known each other from a very early age. For example, male littermates can usually be housed together peacefully as long as there are no sows in the area.

What About Neutering?

You might one day find yourself in a situation where you already own a cavy of one sex and somehow a cavy of the opposite sex finds its way into your home (it happens all the time). To prevent unwanted pregnancies, the animals will have to housed separately, or one of them will have to be neutered before they are placed together in the same cage.

Neutering refers to the removal of some, or all, of the tissues in the body associated with reproduction (testicles in the male, ovaries and uterus in the female). Neutering in the cavy is accomplished surgically (see Chapter Eight, Cavy Health Care).

Should you have the sow spayed (ovariohysterectomy, removal of the uterus and ovaries) or the boar neutered (castration, removal of both testicles)? This is a very important matter to consider and to discuss with your veterinarian. Both procedures can have a significant, and beneficial, impact on your pet's health, behavior, and longevity.

Neutering and spaying are both performed under general anesthesia. Castrating a boar (neutering) is usually less invasive and a more simple procedure than spaying a sow. It is also usually less expensive, and recovery time is shorter. Neutering boars makes them infertile, so the procedure prevents unwanted pregnancies in sows housed together with the boar. Neutering also helps reduce aggression and odor in boars. Because a neutered boar no longer has his testicles, he cannot develop cancer, infection, or other problems of the testicles.

Spaying the sow also has many medical benefits. Ten to twenty percent of sows develop complications during pregnancy, including the need for a C-section. Some cavy pregnancy complications can lead to death. Even if your cavy never gets pregnant, if she is more than three years of age she has a very high chance of developing health problems such as uterine cancer and ovarian cysts. By having your sow spayed while she is young and healthy, you can spare her from these potentially fatal medical conditions and prolong her health and her life.

A Couple or a Crowd?

Keep your animal numbers reasonable so that most of the time you spend with your cavies will be fun time. The number you keep depends on your lifestyle, how much housing space you can provide, whether you want to raise and exhibit cavies, and the amount of time you can dedicate to cultivating your friendship with these charming beings.

Male or Female?

The decision about whether to acquire a boar or a sow depends on your reasons for buying one. If you are simply looking for a wonderful pet and an interesting companion, you will be happy with either one. If you are planning to raise cavies, you obviously need at least one pair to begin your project.

The main physical difference you will note is that the boar is larger (2.1 to 2.6 pounds [950 to1200 g] and 10 inches [25.4 cm] long) than the sow (1.5 to 1.8 pounds [700 to 850 g] and 8 inches [20.3 cm] long). Otherwise, the anatomical differences are subtle. The testicles are retained in the open inguinal canal and mature boars have large testes and obvious scrotal sacs.

Boars and sows have scent (sebaceous) glands, located around the anal area and on the back. Although both males and females rub their scent glands against surfaces as a way of marking territory, males tend to scent-mark more frequently and have a stronger odor.

Why Buy a Baby?

- The ideal age to bring your new cavy home is when he is recently weaned and no longer needs its mother for nutrition, warmth, and protection.
- A baby cavy adapts more readily to its new home and owner.
- The sooner you acquire your cavy, the sooner you can socialize him and integrate him into your family, and the easier it is for the pup to bond with you.
- An older animal has a more difficult time adapting to a change in surroundings, lifestyle, housing, nutrition, and food dishes.
- The earlier you obtain your pet, the more time you will have to share with him and enjoy him.

Some cavy owners think that boars are more lively and sows are more affectionate. Actually, your pet's individual personality has as much, or more, to do with the kind and gentle way he is raised, as it does with his gender. The vast majority of cavies are docile, sweet, social, and affectionate.

Color and Coat Choices

Cavies come in an array of coat types, lengths, colors, and patterns. The American Cavy Breeders Association (ACBA) currently recognizes 13 breeds and 22 varieties (see Chapter Eleven, The Cavy Connoisseur).

Hair length ranges from short and smooth (American), to stiff medium length standing up in rosettes (Abyssinian), to long and straight (Peruvian and Silkie), to curly (Texel), to down-

right kinky or fuzzy (Teddy). Some cavies are a combination of coat colors and types, such as the White-crested, a smooth-coated cavy with a white rosette in the center of its head.

The long-haired, long-maned cavies are elegant and exotic, but it takes work to keep them looking their best in beautiful show condition. They require regular grooming and brushing. Even the shorter-haired breeds need some regular routine grooming. The key word here is "regular." Their grooming doesn't have to be as extensive and time-consuming as the long-haired breeds.

Keep coat color and hair length in mind when you select your pet. A white coat is not easy to keep bright white, and a long flowing coat needs to be kept tangle-free. A smooth, short coat requires regular care and all of the coat types shed regularly. If you don't have the time or desire to do a fair amount of grooming, select a cavy breed and coat type that will be easy to maintain.

Cavy Charm

Every cavy has its own special charm. As you visit caviaries, pet shops, and cavy rescue organizations, in your search for the ideal companion, you will be amazed at the bubbly, cheerful, playful personalities you encounter. Whether you are looking for a lap pet or a show prospect, you will be drawn to one special cavy because of its unique character and qualities. The cavy that radiates a winning personality is the one you will choose to warm your heart.

A Long-term Commitment

How long do cavies live? The life span will vary with each individual animal and the care and nutrition it receives. On average, cavies can live five to six years, and rarely up to eight years. This means a long-term ownership commitment on your part. Although you may have children in the family, or the cavy may be the "child's pet," the fact is, *you* are ultimately responsible for his care.

Never rely on children to take care of the cavy. If you bring a cavy into your life, be prepared to be his caretaker for life. Don't expect children to shoulder the sole responsibility, or to have a continued interest in the animal throughout his long life. Some children will love a pet and care for him faithfully and responsibly for years. For others, the novelty wears off shortly after the animal's arrival. Children change interests, grow up, leave home, and go to college. Cavies live a long time. Be prepared to be the one responsible for your pet's care over the years.

Cavies Grieve, Too

During the life of your endearing pet you will develop a strong emotional attachment to him. When he dies you will experience the heartache that accompanies such a loss. If you already know you want cavies to be part of your life for several years, keep at least two or more at a time. Having more than one cavy will help ease the pain and fill the void when one of the others eventually dies.

Just as you bond with your pet and will miss him when he is gone, your cavy will also grieve for his cagemate if he dies. Cavies have been known to stop eating and drinking when they lose a friend. Under these conditions, your pet's health could rapidly deteriorate. By housing at least three cavies together, your surviving animals will always have each other if the third one should pass away. As unpleasant as it is to talk about the death of a pet, it is important to know that animals also grieve and that there are ways to keep your pet from becoming lonely. It is simply good preventive medicine for your little companion's emotional well-being. He will be happier if he always has a member of his own species to keep him company.

Chapter Four
Housing

Cavies thrived in their native South America for several thousands of years before they became extinct in the wild. Cavies are now domestic house pets. The key words here are "house pets"! Depending on your lifestyle and the amount of time and space you have available, you can design a housing setup in your home that is convenient for you and as complex or simple as you wish. Cavies are easy to please and easy to house safely and comfortably. They will be perfectly happy in most of the wide variety of cage styles available from your local pet store. Or, if you prefer, you can make a custom home for them using readily available material.

Cavies don't need much to turn a cage into "home sweet home," but they do have a few basic requirements: escape-proof housing with a secure door or lid; solid flooring; protection from heat, cold, and drafts; appropriate bedding material; a hideaway for privacy; nutritious food and a water bottle and food dish or feeder; a hay rack; and chew toys.

Housing Considerations

There are some important things to keep in mind when deciding how to house your pet. First, cavies are very social animals, so it is highly recommended that you house at least two together unless you have a lot of free time to spend with your pet to keep it company. A lonely cavy can become bored and depressed. If your pet is too bored, she may develop behavioral problems, such as injuring herself by chewing on her skin and hair; this is called "self-mutilation." Ideally, you should plan from the beginning to provide housing with enough space for at least two animals.

Remember that cavies are rodents and this means that they can chew their way out of almost anything. Chewing is an important rodent activity. The teeth grow continually throughout life and must be worn down by chewing. For this

43

reason, wood and plastic caging are not suitable.

Cavies like to tunnel about in their bedding, but because they are not diggers it is unusual for them to dig their way out of a pen. That doesn't mean other animals can't dig into your pet's enclosure, however. To be on the safe side, your little companion's housing must be made of material strong enough to prevent tunneling and exit or entry.

Wire Floors and Foot Sores

Wire mesh cage floors are not suitable for delicate cavy legs, feet, and toes. Their tiny feet can slip through the wire bottom floor and get caught and injured. Broken hocks and toes are common injuries of cavies housed on wire mesh floors. Crinkle wire mesh is even more damaging to feet than regular wire mesh.

Cavy footpads are bare and sensitive. There is no hair on the bottom of their feet to cushion them against the pressure of a wire floor. Walking on wire mesh is irritating and causes foot sores and ulcerations. Big, heavy, or overweight cavies are most seriously affected.

Wire floors cause problems in addition to sore feet. Research showed that in some breeding herds, breeding cavies housed on wire mesh floors produced 22 percent fewer offspring and their pups weighed 25 percent less at birth. These figures most likely represent stress and pain associated with wire flooring.

Make sure the cage you purchase has a solid bottom floor or floor pan,

Minimum Recommended Cage Size Guidelines

One Cavy
1 foot × 2 feet (31 cm × 62 cm)

Two Cavies
20 inches × 20 inches
(51 cm × 51 cm)

Three Cavies
2 feet × 2 feet (62 cm × 62 cm)

Four Cavies
27 inches × 27 inches
(70 cm x 70 cm)

Five Cavies
2½ feet × 2½ feet
(77 cm × 77 cm)

Spacious Accommodations

If your cavy's cage is spacious enough to accommodate all its animal occupants comfortably with room enough to play and space for hideaways, toys, dishes, and bottles, then you've done a good job.

so that your cavy doesn't develop foot sores. If you must temporarily house your pet in a cage with a wire mesh floor, give it a flat piece of non-resinous wood (that is free of nails, nontoxic, and not chemically treated) to sit on comfortably to protect its dainty feet from injury.

Overcrowding

Cavies are not particularly energetic or lively. Their favorite activities are nibbling, napping, and sitting on laps—activities that don't require a lot of space. So, if they are so calm, why do they require more space than most rodent pets? For one thing, they are larger than most rodents and definitely more rotund. And cavies like to romp and play throughout the day. More important, cavies do not tolerate overcrowding and become very stressed if they are housed in cramped quarters. They need their space!

Cavies are content in a small group of three to five individuals, although you can keep more together if you have enough room. Too many cavies crowded together can become overheated. This is because they do not tolerate heat well. They are good at conserving body heat, but poor at dissipating heat, so the more animals you house together, the warmer they will be. On a warm day, in an overcrowded pen, your pets could heat up to the point that they could die of heatstroke.

Minimum Cage Size Requirements

Ideally, you should allow, at the very least, 2 square feet (.372 m^2) for one cavy and another square foot (.093 cm^2) for each additional animal. For example, two cavies would require 3 square feet (.836 m^2) and three cavies would require 4 square feet (1.5 m^2). However, if you can give your pets more room than this, please do. You will find that when your cavies have enough room, they will leap, hop, twist in the air, and cavort as they play. They will run around the perimeter of the cage and chase each other. The price of a larger cage will be offset by the hours of entertainment your cavies will give you.

Housing Options

The cage, style, and size you select will depend on the number of animals you are housing and the amount of space available in your home.

The type of housing you give your pet is limited only by your imagination. If you keep your cavy indoors and do not have small children or other pets in the house, you may not even need a conventional cage with a lid. A small hard solid plastic child's wading pool (noninflatable) makes a wonderful enclosure without a top. Just be sure the sides are at least

7 inches (18 cm) high so your curious cavy cannot escape. This type of housing is spacious and requires more floor space and more bedding material, but it is practical and easy to clean. The hard plastic surface of the pool is flat and smooth so it is difficult to chew. A child's wading pool can be easily transformed into cavy housing that gives you full view of your pets' activities and lets them have a wider view of their world, too.

Material

Other types of material used for housing are stainless steel, fiberglass, polycarbonate, or durable, smooth, hard plastic that cannot be chewed. These materials are safe and easy to clean and disinfect. Even something as simple as a very large plastic laundry bin can make convenient housing, as long as there is enough space and the walls are not so high or so opaque that your pet's view is totally obstructed. It's no fun being completely "boxed in" and unable to see. You might be able to cut a few windows for your cavies to peek out of and to increase ventilation. Keep the windows small enough and high enough so your pet cannot climb through them or chew on the cut edges.

Not Recommended

• Aquaria

Some people like to use a large Plexiglas aquarium to house baby cavies. This type of housing is not recommended because an aquarium is large, heavy, and cumbersome to clean. Although it provides good visibility and protection from drafts, a Plexiglas aquarium doesn't allow good air exchange or as much ventilation as a cavy needs.

• **Outdoor Housing**

Outdoor temperatures and conditions in most parts of the country for most of the year are not appropriate for cavies. In addition, outdoor predators such as cats, dogs, raccoons, and birds could harm a cavy housed outdoors.

Living Inside

Cavies love living inside your home with you. The moment you come home, your little friend will whistle a greeting to welcome you. And if your clever cavy appears to be catnapping, just try opening the refrigerator door. Your pet is suddenly alert and squealing and whistling, letting you know that she knows exactly where the carrots are kept. These little critters don't miss a thing! They enjoy being a part of your everyday household activities and are a lot of fun when they are kept indoors.

Temperature and Humidity

Place your pet's cage in an area where the humidity is at least 40 percent and preferably 50 to 60 percent (airborne microorganisms that

may cause diseases do not survive well at this humidity). Place the cage in an area where the temperature does not fall below 65°F (18°C) or rise above 75°F (23°C). As the temperature climbs above 75°F, cavies rapidly succumb to heatstroke. At elevated temperatures, male cavies become infertile. Pregnant females are especially prone to heatstroke and death. At 90°F (32.5°C), death can occur rapidly.

Warning: Never place your pet's cage near heaters, radiators, or fans, or in areas of direct sunlight.

Ventilation and Lighting

Fresh air is important. Cavies require well-ventilated (ideally, cavies should have 10 to 15 air changes per hour), but not drafty, enclosures.

If you don't have enough ventilation in your pet's area, purchase a fan to help circulate the air, but don't place the cage too close to the fan.

Although they can tolerate cold temperature better than they can tolerate the heat, cavies are very sensitive to cold, damp, drafty conditions. They are susceptible to respiratory (lung) problems and can quickly develop pneumonia and die. Their housing should be protected from drafts, cold, and dampness.

Cavies are diurnal, meaning they are active during the day. They have peaks of activity in the morning and late afternoon, with intermittent sleep and wakefulness throughout the day. This normal activity is called "crepuscular," from the French word *crépuscule,* which means "twilight." So that your pet can fully enjoy the daytime hours, her cage should be placed in an area of your home that is well lit during the day and dark at night. The best lighting schedule is 12 hours of light during the day and 12 hours of dark at night, but you do not have to follow such a strict schedule if this is not convenient for you.

Bedding Material

Cavy urine is very concentrated and has a strong, distinctive odor. It contains a high concentration of mineral salts and these can form thick deposits (scales) on the cage floor that can be dissolved with vin-

Bedding Material

- Pelleted and shredded paper products make excellent bedding material for cavies.
- Do not use pine or cedar shavings in your pet's cage. Shavings smell nice and look pretty, but they can cause medical conditions such as itchy skin, respiratory problems, and even possible liver problems.
- Avoid wood chips; the sharp pieces can injure your cavy's eyes.
- Avoid sawdust bedding; it is irritating to the lungs, can plug the nostrils, and can dry and damage your pet's eyes.
- Corncob bedding is not recommended because it tends to be very drying to the skin and can be dehydrating, especially for young cavies.
- Do not use cat litter for bedding material, especially clumping or scented products. They are dangerous to your pet's health, especially if ingested.
- Bedding material should be changed at least once a week. If several animals are housed together, bedding may need to be replaced twice a week or more often as necessary.

egar. The ability to concentrate urine makes it possible to retain moisture and certain minerals in the body. It also makes it important to choose the best, cleanest, most absorbent bedding material you can afford.

There are several kinds of bedding material commercially available including wood shavings, recycled shredded or pelleted paper by-products, grass hay, chopped straw, wood chips, sawdust, and corncobs. Every type of bedding has advantages and disadvantages. The kind of cage bedding material you choose depends on convenience, cleanliness, cost, and your cavy's coat type and length.

Paper Products

Pelleted and shredded paper products make excellent bedding material for all cavy breeds, especially for long-haired cavies. Although they can become tangled in the hair, they are easier to comb out than wood shavings. Some cavies have extremely sensitive feet and do better on shredded paper than pelleted paper products because they are softer for their delicate feet.

You can make an excellent bedding combination by layering shredded paper or pelleted paper on the cage floor and covering them with a light layer of grass hay or straw. This provides comfort for your pet and gives it something to nibble on, while keeping it dry and off the absorbent layer below. Be sure to purchase only chopped grass hay or straw, because hay or straw that contain small, sharp, sticklike particles can injure your pet's eyes.

Wood Shavings

Wood shavings smell pleasant and absorb urine and odors, but there are many reasons not to use them. Many cavies will chew on the shavings and eat them and this can lead to serious health problems, such as gastrointestinal obstruction. Some wood shavings have sharp particles and are abrasive and cause pododermatitis, or foot sores. Particles found in wood shavings may get into your pet's eyes and injure them. Fine dust from wood shavings irritates the lungs and leads to allergies—not just for your pets but for you as well. Wood shavings are not suitable for long-haired breeds because they become tangled and matted in the hair and are difficult to remove with a brush or comb.

Many types of wood shavings, such as pine and cedar, contain substances that can cause liver problems, allergies, and skin problems. Use of wood shavings is discouraged, but from a financial point of view, they are usually more affordable than the recommended paper products. If you decide to use wood shavings, use only aspen shavings. These are the safest for cavies.

No matter what type of bedding you select, purchase only products that are packaged and indicated for use as bedding material for caged pets. Shavings, straw, and hay that are sold for use in horse stalls or that are stored in open outdoor bins may be contaminated with undesir-

able material such as urine and germs from wild rodents. They can be a health risk for your cavy and may be a source of rodent disease organisms.

Note: Always make sure that the bedding material you use is as dust-free as possible. Bedding that contains a lot of dust, mold, and fine particles can be very irritating to the lungs and cause wheezing, sneezing, and other respiratory problems.

Keep the Cage Clean

Clean the cage at least once a week, or more often if you have several animals. Cavies are clean animals and they are miserable when their cage is dirty. You'll be miserable too if the odor becomes overpowering. If you can smell it, it's past time to clean it!

The cage and cage floor should be easy to clean, nonporous, and resistant to moisture, salts, and cleansers. You can make a good disinfectant solution by mixing 1 part bleach to 20 parts water.

Warning: Do not use cleaning products that contain phenolics, such as Lysol or Pinesol. These are toxic to cavies.

Be sure to rinse the cage floor pan well with clean water and allow it to dry before adding bedding. The sides of the floor pan should be 3 to 4 inches (8.5 to 11 cm) high to prevent bedding material from spilling out of the cage.

Bottles, Bowls, and Feeders

Fresh water should be available at all times. Cavies are big drinkers— or so it seems. When they are not drinking their water, they're playing in it, so it's not always easy to tell how much they really drink. No matter how much water they normally consume, you have to give them more than they would actually drink because they love to sit in their dish and soil their water. And they won't drink their water if it isn't fresh.

You can tell if your cavy is drinking its water or playing in it by watching your pet closely. When cavies drink from a bowl, they place their front feet on the edge of the dish and tip their heads back after each sip.

If your pet is using a water bowl, be sure to check it several times each day. You will probably have to clean the bowl and replace the water at least twice daily.

Bottles

A water bottle is a good alternative to a bowl and has several advantages. It is less likely to spill or dampen the cage bedding and it can be fastened to the outside of the cage, leaving more cage space available for a play area. A bottle usually holds more water than a dish, reducing the risk that your cavy will run out of water during the day or in the event you are absent from home longer than anticipated. Don't worry if your pet has not used a bottle before; its keen sense of smell will direct it to the water source. It will learn to use the sipper tube immediately.

But be forewarned—cavies find sipper tubes very entertaining. They love to play with them and they waste a lot of water. They also chew on the sipper tubes, especially if the tubes have a ball valve. Be sure the tube is made of metal, not glass or plastic. It's not always easy to tell if your pet is drinking or playing with the tubes. Cavies do not usually lick the tubes, although they can learn to do so. When they are really drinking, they put their mouths around the tube and pull their heads back to draw the water out.

Bottles and sipper tubes have some disadvantages:
• They are more difficult to clean than bowls.
• Sipper tubes can become plugged with food, debris, and bedding material.
• Bacteria grow and multiply in dirty sipper tubes and contaminate the water.

Sipper tubes should be checked daily to be sure they are working properly and cleaned thoroughly each day with a round brush.

Bowls and Feeders

Cavies love to eat, so you might not think feeding them would be very challenging. Think again! They like to forage on the ground, but if you put the food on the floor of the cage, it can be scattered and soiled. It's hard to tell how much is being eaten and how much is wasted.

Hayrack: A hayrack is a good way to keep grass hay and leafy greens clean and fresh. A broad-based or weighted dish or bowl, made of chew-proof material that is safe for rodents, works well for feeding pelleted food. It also makes it easier for you to keep track of your pet's food intake and food preferences.

Feeders: Cavies will readily eat from food bowls, but they seem to spend as much time sitting in them as eating from them. Unfortunately, while they sit in their food dishes they often tip and spill them. Worse yet, they usually defecate and urinate in them, contaminating their food. J-shaped feeders are a good solution because it's hard for an adult cavy to sit in them and the J-shape design makes it more difficult to spill food.

The problem is, cavies are very fussy about how their food is presented and every cavy is different. They each have their own preferences. If they don't like the feeder, dish, bowl, or bottle, they will refuse to eat or drink. So, when you find a feeding and watering method that works for your pets, don't change it.

Hideaways

Every cage should contain at least one hideaway. It can be as simple as a cloth sack, a paper bag, a wooden nest box, a flowerpot, or a large PVC tube. This is where your cavy will spend its private time resting and feeling secure. A hideaway provides the dark and quiet your cavy would experience in an underground burrow. It's a place where it can go and hide when it is frightened or when it wants to have some time alone. When your cavy is tired of all the activity, light, or noise in its environment, it can retreat to its hideaway and relax. Hideaways reduce cage

stress and are an absolute necessity for your pet's health and well-being.

Exercise

Cavies spend most of their time in an awake state, but they are not very dynamic. They need a bit of encouragement to motivate them to exercise and, quite honestly, there's not a lot you can do. Your pet would much rather sit on your lap and munch on some greens than exercise. And who could blame them?

So let's be realistic. Knowing that today's domestic cavy is a creature of comfort, we can at least provide some options that might spike some interest in exercise. We can start by giving them enough cage space to

run and play when they feel like it. And if we house two or more animals together, there is more chance that they will romp and chase each other and take advantage of that extra space when they feel playful.

Most important, your cavy should be allowed at least one hour each day to play in a large play area. This area can be as simple as a small pen set up on your living room floor, as long as the area is safe and you are there to supervise your pet's activities.

Toys for Your Cavy

Cavies are playful animals. They are active year round and do not hibernate. When housed together they spend much of their recre-

Warning: Never give your cavy painted or treated wood.

Other playthings: Cavies appreciate any objects or activities that make life more interesting. They love things they can climb over, push around, or bump with their noses. Toys that dangle or hang from the top of the cage that can be butted around with the nose are especially popular. A simple ball (chew-proof, please!) that can be pushed around the cage makes a great toy. Other favorite playthings include hiding places, nest boxes, and wide, low ramps leading up to large blocks on which to sit. You can buy these items at your local pet store or make many of them yourself. For example, you can create inexpensive tunnels from PVC plumbing pipe from your local hardware store. PVC is safe for your pet, inexpensive, easy to clean, and can be reused. You can also make wooden nest boxes and hid-

ational time simply interacting with each other. Because of their social, inquisitive nature, you should keep your pets in a cage large enough for them to play and socialize and give them plenty of safe, interesting toys. Toys are a worthwhile investment in your little friend's happiness. Cavies love to visit and play and you will love watching them.

Chew toys: Cavies love to nibble and chew. Their teeth grow continually and must be worn down, so they need a constant supply of safe rodent chew toys, such as wooden sticks. It is best to purchase safe rodent chew sticks from the pet store but if you decide to give your pets twigs and sticks, be certain that these materials do not come from any poisonous or potentially harmful plant or tree. Aspen wood makes excellent rodent chew sticks.

Cardboard Tubing

Do not use cardboard tubing from paper towel rolls, toilet paper rolls, or gift-wrapping paper rolls for toys. Although they look like they would make good tunnel toys, most of these tubes (98 to 99 percent) are made from recycled materials and may contain ink residues or other contaminants. Also, some of the glues used to make the cardboard tubes may contain toxins.

ing places from untreated, nontoxic wood. Just keep in mind that whatever types of toys you provide, your cavy will chew on them. Be sure they are made of safe, nontoxic materials.

Often the simplest and cheapest things make the most interesting toys. For example, a simple shower curtain ring attached to the wall of the cage will provide your curious cavy with hours of entertainment. A paper bag gives your pet a place to investigate, crawl into, and tear to pieces. It doesn't take much. Your pet's toy box collection is limited only by your imagination.

Selecting the Perfect Place

Finding just the right location for your pet's cage is important. You have to keep your companion's comfort in mind, as well as your convenience.

• Find a place that is out of direct sunlight. Even if the temperature within your home is comfortable, a cage placed in direct sunlight can heat up rapidly, just like a greenhouse. This is especially true if part of the cage is made of glass or Plexiglas.

• Don't put the cage near a steamy bathroom or close to wood stoves, fireplaces, or heating vents. The inside of the cage can become extremely hot and your cavy could die from heatstroke.

Do not house cavies with or near animals, such as rabbits, cats, and dogs. They may have subclinical (showing no symptoms) infections of *Bordetella* bacteria, which can cause severe disease and illness in cavies.

• Cavies are extremely susceptible to respiratory problems, so make sure to place the cage in an area away from cold, drafts, and air conditioning vents so your pet does not become chilled and develop pneumonia. Baby cavies are particularly sensitive to the cold.

• Put your cavy's home at a comfortable level for viewing and handling. Try to find a location where you can enjoy your pet's activities and be able to reach in to catch it or feed it, clean the cage, change the water bottle, and replace the bedding without having to bend over or stoop.

• Finally, keep your companion's overall environment in mind. Cavies are sensitive and shy. Loud noises frighten them so don't place the cage near the family sound system speakers or television set.

Cavies like to be on the lookout. They want to be sure there are no predators in the area. And they especially want to know when you come home and where you are. Don't obstruct their view by blocking the cage with furniture and walls. Your pet wants to see what's going on!

Chapter Five
Feeding Your Cavy

Cavies love to eat—in fact, they are veritable gourmands. They are also very particular about their food preferences. Unlike many rodents that are omnivorous and will eat almost anything to survive, cavies are strict vegetarians (herbivorous, plant materials only). They are also very selective about what they will consume and they have special nutritional requirements that are quite different from their rodent cousins. Cavies forage throughout the day and consume large quantities of vegetation, including grasses, leaves, and roots. They should always have grass hay and food available. They do not adapt well to limited feeding times.

Cavy Nutrition

Good nutrition plays an important role in your pet's overall health and longevity. If your cavy does not receive proper nutrition or a balanced diet, he can suffer from a variety of health problems, including premature death. The good news is that you have full control of your pet's diet—and it is very easy to provide your little friend a diet that is not only nutritious and balanced, but delicious as well.

Your cavy has special behavioral, anatomical, and biological considerations that influence his dietary needs. For example, his gastrointestinal tract is very sensitive and can be easily upset by a sudden change in diet or the wrong kinds of foods. Special cells, important for the digestion and absorption of food, line the intestinal tract. Bacteria in the gut are important for the absorption of nutrients. If you see your cavy eat his feces, don't be alarmed. This is called coprophagy and is a way cavies and some other animal species "recycle" nutrients, including B vitamins, vitamin K, and some minerals.

As mentioned earlier, a cavy's teeth erupt and grow continuously throughout life. Roughage is necessary in the diet to help keep the teeth worn down and prevents dental problems. Good-quality grass hay is excellent for this purpose and should always be available for your pet. Grass hay provides the necessary roughage your cavy needs.

Scurvy

One of the more remarkable aspects of a cavy's nutritional requirements is the fact that he requires vitamin C (ascorbic acid) in the diet, just as humans do. All other mammals—except humans, nonhuman primates, and some fruit bats—are able to synthesize their own vitamin C and do not need it included in their food. Just as with humans, without adequate vitamin C in their diet, cavies develop "scurvy." This disease causes enlarged chondrocostal junctions, detected as painful lumps along the ribcage, defects in collagen synthesis, abnormalities of bone and teeth, inflamed gums, and eventually death.

Scurvy is the most common nutritional disease seen in cavies, besides obesity. It is also the easiest to prevent. Just be sure your pet receives plenty of vitamin C in its diet.

Commercial Guinea Pig Food

There are several excellent pelleted guinea pig foods available on the market. Be sure the guinea pig food you select contains at least 18 to 20 percent protein, 3 to 4 percent fat, 13 to 16 percent fiber, and at least 0.2 to

Except for scurvy, nutritional disorders are rare in cavies fed a complete and balanced commercial diet.

Food Consumption Guideline

As a general rule, an adult cavy should eat about 6 percent of its body weight in food per day. For example, a 2-pound (1-kg) cavy should eat approximately 2 ounces (60 g) of food every day.

Growing cavies need more nutrition and eat about 8 percent of their body weight in food every day.

0.5 ounce of vitamin C per pound (1 to 3 g vitamin C per kg) of feed.

As you can see, nutrition is a complicated subject. Dietary requirements vary from animal to animal. So how can you be sure your cavy is getting everything he needs in a balanced diet? Make sure that the majority of your pet's diet consists of commercial guinea pig food.

Supplementing

Commercial guinea pig foods contain the ingredients necessary for your pet's health and—except for vitamin C—you do not need to supplement. It's good to leave the challenge of vitamin supplementation to the experts. The minimum dietary requirement for each vitamin has not yet been established for cavies and there is a wide range for some that have been determined; for example, a cavy should receive anywhere from 1.5 mg to 6 mg of vitamin E each day. Commercial guinea pig food companies do a good job of covering

Food	Amount to Feed	Advantages	Disadvantages
Pelleted commercial guinea pig food	One ounce (30–35 g) of pellets per pound (.45 kg) of body weight for adult animals. Increase amount two to three times for growing, pregnant, or lactating animals.	Convenience, nutritionally balanced	Vitamin C in the feed can lose 50 percent of its potency within six weeks; vitamin C in the water can lose 50 percent of its potency within 24 hours.
Grass hay	Unlimited	Helps wear down teeth and provides roughage	Increases vitamin C requirements; can be contaminated with disease-causing organisms (from wild rodents or mold) causing allergy, pneumonia, cancer, or infection; is messy in the home.
Alfalfa hay	One small cube every two to three weeks for maintenance	High in protein	Excess intake can lead to excessive calcium in the urine (hypercalciuria) and cause urinary tract problems.
Leafy, dark green vegetables: kale, parsley, broccoli	Not to exceed 10 percent by weight of the pelleted diet. Limit all treats to one tablespoon (15 ml) in a 24-hour period.	Rich in vitamin C	May be contaminated with pesticides, parasites, or bacteria (*Yersinia, Salmonella*)
Fruits: kiwi fruit, orange	½ teaspoon (2.5 g) weekly	Optional source of vitamin C	Excess sweets can cause weight problems and diabetes.

the bases without the risk of over- or undersupplementing the diet.

Freshness

Be sure the food you provide is fresh. To ensure the freshness of the guinea pig food you purchase, check the milling date on the food package to verify the shelf life of the product. If the food is old, the vitamins in the food will lose their potency and no longer be effective. This is especially true for vitamin C. Although standard laboratory recommendations are to provide food that is no older than six months (180 days) from the time of milling, you should definitely discard any food that is more than 90 days old from the milling date. This is because once the package has been opened and the food has been exposed to atmospheric conditions, vitamin C begins to lose its potency very rapidly. In fact, 50 percent of the vitamin C activity in the feed is lost within six weeks of milling. (Most

- Feed fresh, dark green, leafy vegetables to the diet daily.
- Make sure the guinea pig food you purchase is fresh.
- Store your cavy's food in a closed container in a cool, dark, well-ventilated place.

research laboratories will not feed guinea pig food that is older than four to six weeks of manufacture date.)

Vitamin C (Ascorbic Acid)

The importance of vitamin C in your cavy's diet cannot be overemphasized. Don't worry about overdosing your pet. Extra vitamin C will not harm your cavy, but insufficient vitamin C can be fatal. Vitamin C is not toxic to your pet. Cavies cannot store vitamin C in their bodies for long periods of time; any excess is excreted in the urine. Your pet needs vitamin C on a daily basis, not once a week or once a month.

Although you will be feeding a quality commercial guinea pig food, play it safe. It's not unusual for pet food to sit on the shelf in the stores for several weeks and sometimes the milling date of the product is not easy to locate or decipher on the package. Supplement your cavy daily to make sure he receives enough vitamin C to stay healthy:

- One of the best ways to do this is by feeding leafy, dark green vegetables rich in vitamin C, such as kale, chicory, and parsley.

• Another good way is to add vitamin C to the drinking water.

• You can purchase vitamin C tablets from your pharmacy or vitamin C drops at your local pet store. Make sure the tablets or drops contain *only* vitamin C. You may accidentally overdose your pet on other vitamins if you buy a multivitamin mix.

Laboratory research recommendations for vitamin C supplementation range from 50 mg vitamin C per cup (8 ounces [240 ml]) of drinking water, up to 1 g of vitamin C per quart (32 ounces [960 ml]) of water. You can easily stay within this range by crushing a 250 mg (for the lower dose range), 500 mg (for a medium dose), or 1,000 mg (for the higher recommended dose) tablet of vitamin C and adding it to one quart (960 mL) of water.

Remember that vitamin C is unstable when exposed to air or certain components in hard tap water. In warm environments vitamin C will lose half of its potency in the

The Missing Enzyme

Why can't cavies make their own vitamin C to meet their bodies' needs?

Cavies are unique animals. Unlike most other mammals, cavies do not have the enzyme L-gluconolactone oxidase, needed to manufacture vitamin C from glucose in the body.

water within 24 hours, so be sure to provide fresh bottled distilled or deionized water (purchased from the supermarket) with fresh vitamin C added daily.

Cavies have discriminating tastes. Your pet might dislike the flavor of water supplemented with vitamin C and refuse to drink it. Monitor your pet's water consumption closely. If your cavy stops drinking, immediately discontinue adding vitamin C to the water. It's hard to believe, but if your cavy objects to the vitamin taste, it will refuse to drink and could allow itself to die of thirst.

When adding vitamin C to the drinking water, remember:

1. Use only bottled deionized or distilled water purchased from the supermarket. Vitamin C is destroyed by tap water from copper plumbing.

2. Do not use carbonated water.

3. Use only stainless steel or Pyrex (not glass) sipper tubes.

4. Change the water daily and add new supplement daily.

5. Watch the water level in the bottle or bowl closely to be sure your cavy is drinking and immediately discontinue vitamin C supplementation in the water if your pet refuses to drink because it doesn't like the taste.

6. Do not rely entirely on vitamin C supplementation in the water to fulfill your pet's dietary needs.

Tablets: Some cavies will eat a vitamin C tablet directly, or crumbled on the food pellets. Be sure to sup-

plement your cavy with a minimum 90 mg of vitamin C every day.

The Other Vitamins

Vitamins are essential to your pet's health, but an excess intake of some vitamins can be as harmful as a deficiency. Not all vitamins need to be added to the diet. For example, it is believed that vitamin K and B vitamins are "recycled" through coprophagy.

A Menu for Cavies

Cavies are eager eaters, but their appetite doesn't always correlate with their activity level.

Food intake varies with life stage, activity level, and age. A good guideline is to allow 1 ounce (30 to 35 g) of commercial pelleted guinea pig food per pound (.45 kg) of body weight for an adult. If your small companion is rather rotund and sedentary, you may have to feed less. For an active, growing, or pregnant animal, you will

Rabbit, Mouse, or Rat Food

Never feed rabbit, mouse, or rat food to your cavy. These foods are not the correct size, firmness, and consistency for cavies (they are usually too large and firm). They will not fulfill your pet's dietary needs. More important, they do not contain the necessary vitamin C that cavies require for life. In addition, rabbit foods contain too much vitamin D for cavies and can cause serious health problems.

Vitamin Supplements

Vitamin	Minimal Daily Requirement	Nutritional Disease	Symptoms
Vitamin C (ascorbic acid)	5 mg per pound of body weight (10 mg per kg) for maintenance and 15 mg per pound of body weight (30 mg per kg) during pregnancy	"Scurvy" caused by insufficient intake of vitamin C on a daily basis	Pain, enlarged chondrocostal junctions (lumps along ribcage), defects in collagen synthesis, abnormal bone, teeth, inflamed gums, death
Vitamin A	Not established	Hypervitaminosis A (excess vitamin A) in the diet	Birth defects, soft tissue and skeletal abnormalities
Vitamin D	Not established	Hypovitaminosis D (inadequate vitamin D in diet)	Abnormal growth and development of bones and teeth. (Commercial rabbit food contains too much vitamin D for guinea pigs.)
Vitamin E	Not established; considered to be between 1.5 and 6 mg per day	Hypovitaminosis E (inadequate vitamin E in diet)	Degeneration of skeletal muscles, partial paralysis, reproductive problems, and fetal death
Vitamin K	Not established; dietary vitamin K considered unnecessary, probably because vitamin K is "recycled" through coprophagy		
B vitamins B^6	Not established; may not be necessary because B vitamins are "recycled" through coprophagy		
Folic Acid	2 to 3 mg/kg food for young guinea pigs. 3 to 6 mg/kg body weight for young guinea pigs		

have to double or triple that amount. Observe your pet closely every day to be sure that he is not too thin or too heavy and adjust his ration of food accordingly and *gradually*.

Note: Invest in a baby scale to weigh your cavy once a week. The best way to know if your pet is eating the right amount of food is if he is the right weight (not too heavy and not too thin) and acting healthy.

The ideal cavy diet is a correct balance of nutrients—protein, fat, carbohydrate, vitamins, minerals, and water—fed in just the right amount for your pet's stage in life: growth, maintenance, reproduction, or old age. A combination of commercial guinea pig food, some fresh leafy greens, vegetables, unlimited grass hay, and a little bit of fruit make it easy to create the perfect delectable diet for your little friend.

Here are some things to keep in mind when you create your cavy's menu:

• Cavies will eat a lot of different plant foods, but they usually do not like salty, sweet, or bitter foods. If you want to give a special "treat," try some dandelions; these are a cavy delicacy. But only feed your pet a few as too many can cause diarrhea.

• Hay supplementation is an important part of the diet. It helps keep the teeth worn down and satisfies the need to chew. It also provides roughage necessary for digestion.

• Feed your cavy unlimited fresh grass hay daily; cavies love alfalfa, but it is very rich and fattening and eating too much can lead to health problems.

• Health problems have been linked to feeding the wrong kinds of hay.

Do not feed coarse hay that can injure the tissues of the mouth and cause bacterial infections.

Do not feed hays that are rich in substances (oxalates) that cause urinary tract stones.

Basic Feeding Guidelines

It's easy to feed your cavy a nutritional, healthy diet if you follow some basic guidelines:

1. Feed a complete balanced commercial guinea pig food that meets your pet's special nutritional needs.
2. Don't feed any foods that are not suitable for cavies.
3. Don't overfeed your pet.
4. Supplement your cavy's diet with vitamin C daily.

Food Consumption	Water Intake	Urine Output
Approximately 1 ounce (28.35 g) per pound (453 g) of body weight per day	Approximately 2 ounces (60 to 80 ml) per pound (453 g) of body weight per day	Approximately 1 ounce (20 to 25 ml) per adult per day

Do not feed moldy or contaminated hay. It causes poisonings, infections, and even death.

• Your cavy needs at least 16 percent fiber in his commercial diet.

• An increase in roughage increases dietary vitamin C requirements, so supplement accordingly.

• Feed only hay that is clean, dry, and packaged and sold as food for pet rodents.

• There should always be a little bit of leafy vegetables in the feed rack at all times.

• Leafy, dark green vegetables such as kale, parsley, and broccoli are rich in vitamin C but should not exceed 10 percent by weight of your pet's pelleted diet.

• Only fresh vegetables are of nutritional value. Vegetables may be contaminated with pesticides, parasites,

Rinse Your Cavy's Vegetables

Vegetables from the store may be contaminated with bacteria (*Salmonella* and *Yersinia*), parasites, or chemicals and pesticides. Before you feed vegetables to your cavy, make sure they are clean and safe.

- Mix ½ ounce (4 ml) of household bleach in 1 quart (1.14 L) of tap water.
- Soak vegetables for 10 minutes.
- Rinse well.

or bacteria (*Yersinia, Salmonella*), so be sure they are thoroughly cleaned and rinsed before offering them to your cavy.

- Cavies don't enjoy cold vegetables so let them warm up a little after you take them out of the refrigerator before you give them to your pet.
- Hang all leafy greens from a hayrack so they are not stepped on and soiled, and remove all old food from the cage daily.

- Fruit treats provide an additional source of vitamin C, but don't feed too many. They are high in sugar and can cause weight problems, diabetes, and diarrhea.
- Cavies like kiwi fruit, oranges, strawberries, grapes, peaches, apricots, and melons. Limit fruit to ½ to 1 teaspoon (2.5 to 5 g) or less daily and limit all treats to 1 tablespoon (15 g) in a 24-hour period. If your cavy starts to put on too much weight, feed less fruit.
- Alfalfa hay cubes are high in protein. They are also fattening. Too much alfalfa can lead to hypercalciuria and cause urinary tract stones and other problems. Limit alfalfa to one cube every two to three weeks.
- Don't feed your cavy grass clippings. They cause bloat and diarrhea and may contain pesticides.

Finicky Eaters

If you think your pet is set in his ways and has discriminating taste, you're right. A cavy will develop definite food preferences at an early age and once his tastes are established, they will be difficult, if not impossible, to change. Cavies have been known to starve to death because they didn't like the food they were fed and simply refused to eat it.

You can prevent problems by feeding a healthy, balanced diet from the start. It's a good idea to serve a combination of two or three good-quality brands of guinea pig food mixed together at each meal. That way, if one of the brands is no longer carried by your local pet store, or no longer manufactured, you won't have to suddenly change your cavy's diet and run the risk that he will refuse to eat. You will still be able to mix the other two food brands together and your pet may not notice that one brand is missing from the mixture.

Whatever you feed, be consistent. If your cavy is eating a good diet, don't change it unless there is an excellent reason to do so. If you must change the diet, do it gradually. A sudden dietary change can stress your pet so much that he may stop eating and drinking. In fact, once cavies like what they are eating and how it is presented, they don't want anything changed. Even something as simple as changing the food dish can seriously upset your small companion.

If you acquire a cavy that has already developed poor eating habits—he may prefer to eat only treats or fruits—be patient and work with your stubborn little friend. Remove the inappropriate food gradually, a little bit at a time each day, and

Everyone Needs to Eat

If you have more than one cavy, put two or more feeders in the cage so that food is available to all of your cavies. Several feeders help prevent food disputes, too.

Iceberg Lettuce

Iceberg lettuce is notoriously deficient in calcium and also causes diarrhea. When you want to give your cavy a nutritious treat, feed it kale instead of lettuce. Cavies love kale and it's rich in vitamin C (100 g of kale provide 125 mg of vitamin C).

replace it with a small amount of pelleted guinea pig food. Remember that the dietary transition, if successful, may take several weeks and you might have to introduce different types of guinea pig food before you find one your cavy will accept.

Make sure a quality commercial guinea pig food and fresh, leafy, dark green vegetables make up the majority of your pet's diet and don't feed too many snacks, especially those high in sugar content. If your cavy consumes too many treats, he will eat less of his guinea pig food and will not receive a balanced diet.

Harmful Foods

Not all vegetables are good for cavies. Spinach, beet tops, and the green parts of potatoes ("potato eyes") can cause health problems. Beet tops and spinach are rich in oxalates that cause urinary tract problems. Potato greens contain solanine, a toxic ingredient that causes severe gastrointestinal disorders.

Foods to Avoid

Moldy hay, soiled hay
Health Problems: Disease of the lymph nodes, pneumonia, infections
Toxic Substance or Organism: Fungal organisms: *Absidia ramosa, Absidia corymbifera, Aspergillus fumigatus* and plant estrogens

Peanuts
Health Problems: Lethargy, obesity, poisoning
Toxic Substance or Organism: Aflatoxins

Lettuce
Health Problems: Diarrhea, lethargy
Toxic Substance or Organism: Laudanum

Spinach, beet tops
Health Problems: Urinary tract problems and stones
Toxic Substance or Organism: Oxalates

Potato greens
Health Problems: Digestive upset, poisoning
Toxic Substance or Organism: Solanine

Note: Remember to wash vegetables thoroughly to remove all traces of chemicals or pesticides before adding them to the meal.

Don't give your cavy any foods that can cause gas production, such as onions (toxic to many pets) and garlic. Cavies like broccoli and cabbage, but they can cause gas in some individuals. Cabbage is rich in vitamin C but it is also rich in oxalates and can contribute to urinary tract problems if your cavy eats too much of it. If you decide to feed these vegetables, start out with just a tiny amount first and see how your pet does.

Never feed your cavy chocolate, which contains theobromine, a product similar to caffeine, or other candies. Avoid feeding cooked or processed foods, which may be lacking in vitamins or contain food additives and preservatives.

If you are not sure about the safety or nutritional benefit of any food type, simply do not feed it to your pet.

Playing with Food

Cavies love to play with their food; they also waste a lot of it. It's a cavy conundrum we must learn to accept. No matter what you do, your cavy will find a way to play in its food, spill its food, dig in or sit in the dishes and feeders, and defecate and urinate in them. And of course, soiled food must be replaced frequently, at least twice a day.

Feeders and Dishes

You can prevent some of the wastage by purchasing feeders and dishes that are difficult to sit in or tip. For example, some dishes have lips along the top that curve inward, reducing spillage. A heavy, lead-free, no-spill crock is difficult to tip. The problem with large crocks is that they are easy to climb into and your pet can soil a large amount of food. They are also easy to dig in and your cavy can spill and waste food as he searches for a choice morsel. If you use a crock or dish, use the smallest size possible for convenient feeding. This will minimize wastage. Feeders (J-shaped feeders) that attach to the outside of the cage are handy because they do not take up cage floor space and most adult cavies cannot fit in or sit in them.

Amount to Feed

Take food wastage into account when you figure out how much to feed your pet. Each animal is different and some are more wasteful than others. By measuring the amount of food that is lost each day, you can accurately determine how much food you need to provide. Feed your cavy the amount he needs to maintain his ideal body weight, plus the amount of food he wastes daily.

If you are housing two or more animals together, feeding becomes more challenging. Some animals will eat more and others will waste more. You will have to provide extra food to compensate. Be sure to check your pets daily to be sure one or more is not becoming overweight or too thin. If they are, you may have to house them separately, but in cages side by side so they don't become lonely. This way you can observe and control their individual food and water intake.

Cavies are creatures of habit. They may play messy in their dishes, but

they are fastidious eaters. They will readily eat out of a dish, a crock, a bowl, or feeder. Once they are accustomed to the way their food is served, they will object to any change. In fact, switching to a different food bowl or feeder can upset your pet so much that he may refuse to eat. Cavies have been known to starve to death, simply because they refused to eat from a different dish. So decide on a convenient feeding method and stick to it. Don't make any changes unless absolutely necessary.

Water

Depending on where you live, contents of city or well water may vary and could contain additives such as chlorine and chloramine, or high levels of undesirable elements, such as arsenic, or low levels of bacteria. Even if your water doesn't contain these ingredients, it still might taste bad. If the water tastes unpleasant to you, your cavy will probably turn up his nose at it too. And if you have a water softener in your home, the water may contain high levels of salt that are bad for your pet's health.

The best water you can give your pet is the same drinking water you filter or buy for yourself. Commercial bottled drinking water is an inexpensive and safe way to ensure the health of your pet.

Amount of Water

Cavies are very messy drinkers and they drink a lot of water, so plan on at least 1 ounce of water for every ounce of body weight (100 ml per 100 g body weight). When given a choice, cavies prefer to drink out of water crocks, but ideally you should give them water in a bottle. Water in crocks or dishes become soiled with bedding and feces; water in bottles stays cleaner longer. Make sure your playful, water-loving friend has at least 1 pint (473 ml) of fresh, pure, clean drinking water at all times.

Water consumption depends on your pet's health, condition, age, and ambient conditions. A dry diet also increases the need for water and much of your pet's diet consists of dry pellets.

Fluid intake is also greatly influenced by activity level and reproductive cycle. If your cavy is pregnant, or nursing babies, she can easily drink more than twice the amount of water she usually does. Room temperature and humidity also affect how much water your pet consumes. Animals housed in a warm, dry room will drink more than those in cooler, more humid environments.

Always give more water than your cavy normally drinks. If you are housing several animals together, be sure the water supply is sufficient to provide the animals all the water they will need, plus some extra, and make sure the sipper tube is within the animals' reach. If your cavies are drinking from water bottles, make sure you have enough bottles to provide at least 1 pint (473 ml) of water for each animal in the cage. Remember that cavies love to play with everything, especially their sipper tubes. This results in water loss, so keep a close eye on the water level.

Sipper Tubes

Check the sipper tube daily to make sure it is working properly and is not plugged. Many animal deaths have been due to sipper tubes that were plugged with bedding material or debris, denying water access to a thirsty pet.

If you have baby cavies, they should also have access to the sip-

per tube. Although their mother will nurse them for two to three weeks, they will begin to drink water and eat solid food within a few days of birth. Lower the water bottle so that the sipper tube is 1 to 2 inches (2.5 to 5 cm) above the cage floor, within reach of the pups. It should not be so low that it comes in contact with the cage bedding. If this happens, the sipper tube can either become plugged or the water may completely leak out into the bedding material. Bacteria rapidly multiply in sipper tubes plugged with debris and contaminate the water.

Cleaning Bottles and Sipper Tubes

Clean your cavy's bottles and sipper tubes with a mild detergent, like the one you use for your own dishes. Rinse them thoroughly to completely remove all traces of the detergent. You can also soak the bottle and sipper tube for a few minutes in mildly chlorinated water, then rinse them thoroughly, several times. If you prefer, you can use boiling water to rinse the water bottle and soak the sipper tube. When the water bottle and sipper tube are rinsed well and completely cooled, fill the water bottle with commercial bottled drinking water sold for human consumption.

Remember:
- Check your cavy's water bottle several times daily.
- Be certain the sipper tube is not plugged and is working properly.
- Make sure the sipper tube is within reach, especially for baby cavies.

Chapter Six

Your Cavy Comes Home

At last—the day you have been dreaming of and planning for has come. You've found the perfect cavy and it's time to bring her home! Everything has to be in tip-top condition for the new arrival, so let's make sure nothing has been overlooked.

Selecting a Veterinarian

Cavies are generally hardy animals that do very well with good care and nutrition. However, if your pet becomes sick or injured, you will need to take her to your veterinarian for an examination and possible treatment. If you own several cavies, and one of them is sick, it is important to determine the cause of illness to be sure that the problem is not contagious to you or your other pets.

Many veterinarians specialize in small mammals, or have a special interest in them. Cavies have nutritional, housing, and medical requirements that are very different from the larger companion animals. They are very sensitive to certain products and medications used for treating more common pets.

Don't forget to make a list of all the questions and topics you want to discuss with your veterinarian. That way you won't forget to ask something important and you can make the most of every minute of your consultation.

It is a good idea to contact veterinarians *before* your pet needs veterinary care. This gives you an opportunity to introduce yourself as a possible future client and meet the veterinarians in your area who have an expertise in cavies. You can then decide *beforehand* where you would take your cavy if she becomes ill, and not be burdened with the decision during an emergency situation.

You and your veterinarian will be partners sharing responsibility for ensuring your companion's health throughout her life. For this reason, you should be as particular about choosing a veterinarian as you are about selecting your own doctor. Fortunately, there is no shortage of excellent veterinarians, but how do you find the veterinarian that's just right for you and your pet?

Here are some guidelines to help you in the selection process:

• Find a veterinarian who appreciates cavies as much as you do and who is familiar with them.

A great way to find an excellent veterinarian who loves cavies and is very knowledgeable about their special medical needs and care is to contact the Association of Exotic Mammal Veterinarians (AEMV). You may find veterinarians who are AEMV members by visiting the AEMV website (*www.aemv.org*) and clicking on Member Veterinarians, and then entering your state and clicking Get Vets. This will then display a list of AEMV member veterinarians in your state.

If there are no AEMV member veterinarians in your area, you may contact your local county veterinary medical association and ask the executive director there for a list of veterinarians in your area who treat and have a special interest in exotic mammal pets. You may also contact your state board of veterinary examiners and ask them for a list of veterinarians who treat exotic mammal pets.

Finally, if you live in a state that has a veterinary college, and you live near the veterinary college, there are always specialists in exotic mammal medicine at the veterinary college teaching hospital who would be eager to help you with your cavy.

• Ask satisfied cavy owners and members of the local cavy clubs which veterinarians they recommend in your area. Word of mouth is one of the best ways to find a veterinarian.

• Consider convenience. What are the doctors' office hours, schedule, and availability? Who is available on weekends and holidays, or in case of emergency? How close is the veterinary clinic or hospital? Will you be able to travel there within a reasonable amount of time in the event of an emergency?

• What are the fees for services? Most veterinarians provide a price estimate for anticipated services and expect payment when service is provided. Be sure to ask what types of payment methods are available.

• Make an appointment to tour the veterinary hospital facilities. Examine all of the hospital during your tour, particularly as it concerns cleanliness and odors. Does it have special hospital facilities and equipment for tiny animals?

You and your veterinarian will develop a relationship of mutual respect and trust. You will rely on each other for accurate information and work together as a team. The chemistry between you and your veterinarian must be just right.

The first veterinary visit should take place within 48 hours of purchasing your pet. Most breeders and pet stores offer a health guarantee, ranging from 48 hours to one week, depending on the seller. Take advantage of this opportunity to take your cavy to the veterinarian for an examination. During that time period, if she

has a problem or becomes ill, you can return her for a full reimbursement if you desire, or begin medical treatment if necessary.

The veterinary visit is a good time to get answers to any questions you have about your new pet. It's a time to discuss your cavy's special needs, the breeder's or pet store's recommendations, and to plan a complete health care program. Take advantage of the visit to discuss nutrition. Your veterinarian will make an assessment and keep a record of your cavy's health. If there are any changes in the future, a comparison can be made that will be helpful in determining the progression or improvement of your pet's condition at the time.

Preparing for the Trip Home

Make sure you have everything you need for your new pet: a spacious cage in a good location, nutri-

tious food, bottles, dishes, toys, and hideaways. Have your cavy's house all set up in advance so that when you get home you can simply transfer the animal directly into her new environment and she won't have to wait, confused and uneasy, in the carrying case while you get everything ready.

Buy a comfortable carrying kennel or crate to transport your pet—one that is escape-proof and well ventilated. A small flight kennel, like the ones designed for cats or ferrets, will work well and can later serve as a hideaway, if there is space for it within your pet's enclosure.

Cover the carrying kennel with a light towel to block out some of the loud sounds and bright lights that might frighten your little traveler while she is being transported. Just be sure there is plenty of ventilation and air in the kennel.

Be sure to ask the breeder or pet store what type of food the animal has been eating and buy some of the same kind before you bring your pet

home. That way your cavy won't suffer the stress, in addition to a change of environment, or a change in diet.

It's best to take your pet straight home from the breeder's or pet store. The only stop you should be making on the way home is at the veterinarian's. However, if you do need to stop for any reason, *remember to never leave your cavy in a parked car on a warm day, even for a few minutes*. The temperature inside a car, even with the windows cracked open and parked in the shade, can quickly soar past 120°F (49°C) within a few short minutes and your pet can rapidly overheat and die of heatstroke.

Safety First

Before you bring your pet home, go through your house thoroughly one more time and look for any possible hazards an inquisitive cavy could encounter if it were to accidentally escape. Look for any spaces or holes that it could crawl or fall into and be trapped. You might not think of it that way, but your house is a dangerous jungle for a cavy. Let's take a look at some of the many accidents waiting to happen in your home so you can prevent them *before* they occur.

Sticky Traps, Snap Traps, and Rodent Poisons

Remove all sticky traps and snap traps that are in your house or garage. Throw away any rodent bait or poison that may have been left out for wild vermin. They are as deadly for your pet as they are for wild rodents.

Household Chemicals

Cavies can hide in cabinets where there are often household products such as cleaning agents, bug sprays, paints, fertilizers, pesticide baits, and other poisonous chemicals. All of these substances are extremely dangerous and potentially deadly for your cavy if she comes in contact with them. Some types of paints can be toxic to your pet if she chews on wooden baseboards or walls.

Electrical Shock

If your cavy escapes in the house, unplug and remove any electrical cords that may be within her reach. Electrocution from gnawing on an electrical cord is a real potential danger. It could cost your pet her life and possibly cause an electrical fire in your home.

Appliances

Before you do the laundry, check any piles of clothing you have lying on the floor and double-check the pockets. Sadly, more than one small pet has been found, too late, inside the washer or dryer. This type of accident is less likely for a large cavy, but it is a real risk for a youngster.

Be very careful when you vacuum under and behind furniture. If you have a powerful built-in vacuum system in your home, and if the vacuum extension has been removed, a baby cavy could easily be sucked down the vacuum hose.

Pets

Other pets in the house can pose a serious threat to your cavy. A gentle dog, a fun-loving ferret, or a curious cat quickly regains its instincts to hunt or kill small prey, especially when stimulated by the sight of a small animal trying to flee. A fatal accident can take place in a split second. And if your cavy finds a safe hiding place, there is less chance of her coming out if she hears and smells other animals in the area. Until your cavy is recovered, put your other pets in a secure place where they cannot hurt her when she does finally come out of hiding.

If there are small children in the house, ask their assistance in finding your cavy. Children are very eager to be helpful and are remarkably skilled at finding things. But remind the child not to touch the animal when she is found. Although cavies are not prone to biting, if they are startled or mishandled they can inflict serious bite wounds. Also, a small child may inadvertently frighten your pet away before you arrive and capture her.

Outside Doors

Make sure all doors to the outside or the garage are closed. If your cavy escapes to the garage, she will be exposed to additional hazards and poisons. For example, she might find a few drops of antifreeze (ethylene glycol) on the garage floor. Antifreeze has a sweet taste that appeals to animals, but is a deadly poison that causes kidney failure in a very short time. If your pet escapes to the outdoors, she will be virtually impossible to find and she will certainly not survive the dangers of automobiles, neighborhood animals, wild birds, and harsh weather conditions.

Poisonous Plants

While your little herbivore is on the loose she may get hungry and what could be more appetizing than some greenery? Unfortunately, many household and garden plants are poisonous, so be sure to remove any plants, as well as fertilizers and pesticides, that could make your cavy sick.

Some common poisonous plants include

• Aconite
• Amaryllis
• American Holly
• American Nightshade
• Angel's Trumpet
• Azalea
• Bird of Paradise
• Birdseye Primrose
• Blue Cardinal Flower (Lobelia)
• Buttercup (Ranunculus)
• Crocus
• Chrysanthemum

• Daffodil
• Daily
• Foxglove (Digitalis)
• Hydrangea
• Iris
• Lily (several species of lily)
• Lupine
• Mistletoe
• Monkshood
• Oleander
• Onion
• Philodendron
• Poinsettia
• Rhododendron
• Tulip
• Wolfsbane
• Yew

Crushing Injuries

Once you have an escapee in the house, everyone must pay close attention to where they step. Your cavy can be underfoot before you know it. Cavies like to hide in dark places, so inspect your closets and the insides of shoes and boxes. Be careful where you step and where you sit down.

Capturing Your Cavy

If your cavy is loose in the house, and you can't find her, you might be able to capture her by setting her cage, nest box, or travel kennel on the floor. Leave the door open and bait the inside with a favorite treat, then leave the area. It helps to turn down the lights and be very quiet. This helps your cavy to calm down after the excitement of her free run of the house.

If your pet is tired and hungry and is hiding nearby—and if you are very lucky—she may return to her home to eat and rest. Your cavy would rely on her keen sense of smell more than her eyesight to find her way home. Unfortunately, if your cavy has wandered into a distant part of the house, she probably doesn't have a clue where to go to find her cage. Unlike rats and mice, cavies are not experts at finding their way through a maze, so you can imagine what it's like for them to find their way through your home.

Don't expect your pet to come home on her own. She most probably will not. It's up to you to actively search for your lost pet before she gets into trouble. Be prepared to capture your cavy when you do find her. If your pet is very tame and recognizes you, you can probably approach her slowly and gently scoop her up in your hands. Just in case, it's helpful to have a tightly woven fish or butterfly net with a long handle available in case she decides to bolt and you need help capturing

her. If you don't have a net you can use a small sheet or towel to throw over your pet. Once the cloth is over the animal, you must act quickly to roll up the cavy in the material and transfer her to her cage. Be gentle so you don't hurt her. You can also try using a box to place over your cavy, but this can be cumbersome and you might accidentally injure your pet in the process.

Traps

Another option is to purchase a small humane trap, such as a Havahart trap, at the local pet shop or feed store, or you may be able to rent or borrow one from your local animal shelter or veterinarian. (If you rent a trap, disinfect it thoroughly before you use it. It may have been used to trap sick or wild animals and could have germs on it that are dangerous to your pet.)

Bait the trap with your cavy's favorite treat (carrots, apples, oranges, and dandelions are very popular) and place it in an easily accessible and quiet area. Cavies are very reluctant to enter places they do not know, so a successful trapping isn't guaranteed.

You are most likely to catch your pet during the day when she is most active. She will probably be hidden and napping during some of the night.

Check your traps several times a day. By the time you catch your cavy she may be very hungry and thirsty and may need immediate care.

Never pick a cavy up by the scruff, or nape, of the neck. Cavies have large pelvic girdles and their rump and hind legs must be supported at all times.

How to Hold and Cuddle a Cavy

Cuddling is one of the things cavies do best. All you have to do is pick them up carefully and gently, and make sure they don't squirm loose or fall. It's that simple.

Babies: To properly pick up a baby cavy, cup both of your hands together and scoop the baby up under the rump and into the palms of your hands. Close your hands firmly, but not tightly, around the baby and hold it close to your chest.

Adults: To pick up an adult cavy, gently slip your hand under the chest and belly and allow it to place its feet on the palm of your hand and your forearm. Place your other hand over the top of the animal to support it and keep it from falling. Bring the animal up close against you and

hold it gently and well supported, with both hands.

Another method is to grasp the cavy around its shoulders with one hand and lift it securely but gently, while supporting the hindquarters in the opposite hand. Be very careful not to hold or squeeze too tightly around the chest because you can accidentally damage the fragile tissues of the lungs. Hold your pet close against your chest with both hands to prevent it from falling.

If your pet squirms and is difficult to hold, put her back down or bring her up against your chest or hold her on your lap. Talk to her in a calm, soothing voice until she stops wiggling. The one thing you must not do is let her drop or fall. When cavies are dropped, they almost always are seriously injured. Broken backs, legs, and feet are usually caused by falling or dropping, even from a short distance.

One way to calm your pet is to offer her a small treat. Cavies are easily distracted and reassured by a tasty morsel. And if you prefer to hold your cavy in your lap, a piece of kale or carrot will keep her glued to the spot.

Social Skills and the Congenial Cavy

The more time you spend with your pet, the more sociable she will be. She will quickly learn to recognize you and demand attention from you by whistling and calling to you.

Cavies enjoy being caressed and will "purr" or "churr" and chatter their teeth when petted. This means they love the attention and are having a good time.

Your cavy will love spending time on your lap, but don't always expect the best manners. It's a good idea to always keep a little towel spread over your lap when you hold your pet, just in case she has an "accident" and has to urinate or defecate. Cavies don't give any warning; these things just happen, so it's best to take precautions.

Never try to discipline your cavy or teach her "social skills," manners, or tricks. Your small friend is limited in how much she can learn and understand. A cavy cannot be completely housebroken like a dog and should not be punished if it soils an area. It doesn't know any better and cannot be trained to time its natural body functions. It also cannot be trained to come when you call it or to go to its cage on command.

On the other hand, your pet is extremely sociable and endowed with a gentle nature, calm disposition, and endearing appearance. Unless frightened or injured, she doesn't try to bite, scratch, roam, or run

away. She is quiet and she doesn't annoy the neighbors. She makes a wonderful, affectionate, cuddly companion. It's easy to overlook your pet's few "shortcomings" when her list of qualities is endless.

Warning: A cavy should never be punished in any way. Never strike or hit a cavy. Never shout at a cavy.

Chapter Seven

Understanding Your Cavy

Scientists have been intrigued with cavy behavior since they started to study it more than a century ago. The problem is, we don't have a lot of information about the lifestyle of our domestic cavy when it was a wild animal. It has been domesticated for so long that we know little about its social organization, predators, and way of life outside of captivity. There are, unfortunately, no *Cavia porcellus* left in the wild for us to study and answer our questions.

Our knowledge of domestic cavy behavior is based on what we see at home and in research laboratories. We study the behaviors of the domestic cavy's wild relatives and take everything into consideration. We analyze and make comparisons. We extrapolate and contemplate. For example, we know that cavies in the wild did not dig tunnels and preferred to live in burrows already created and abandoned by other animals. We see the same characteristics in our small companions. They do not dig and although they enjoy hideaways, they won't tunnel

and create their own hiding places; we have to provide them.

By studying cavy behavior, we can draw some conclusions about how cavies lived in the wild thousands of years ago, the kinds of behaviors they show today, why they do the things they do, and how we can take better care of them.

The cavy's behaviors and ways of communicating reflect millions of years of ancestral development coupled with thousands of years of domestication—an interesting combination that makes for interesting observations.

The Contented Cavy

It's easy to know when your cavy feels comfortable and secure. His sense of well-being is contagious as he literally frolics in his cage, bucking like a miniature bronco, shaking his head, leaping and twisting in the air, running in circles around his cage, chasing his friends, grooming, napping, and snacking. All of

these activities are signs of a happy, healthy cavy.

Grooming

After eating, or when your pet feels calm and comfortable, he will groom himself. He will start by licking his front feet and wiping his face, then sitting on his haunches and bringing both front feet over the head from behind the ears, all the way down to the tip of his nose. The chest is cleaned with the teeth and tongue, back and forth, while the front feet groom and push the hairs on the sides of the body. He will scratch his body with his hind feet and clean his toenails with his teeth. When your cavy is finished grooming himself, he will usually vigorously shake all over, as if to remove loose hairs and fluff out the coat. There is a set routine in the grooming pattern and you will learn to recognize your cavy's own grooming style.

Note: If your cavy doesn't groom himself, it is a sure sign that he doesn't feel well.

Unlike many rodent species, cavies do not spend time grooming each other. The mother cavy will clean her babies' anogenital area, but mutual grooming doesn't go beyond that.

The Cavy Community

The cavy's success as a house pet is due in large part to its highly social behavior. The more sociable an animal is, the more appealing it is as a pet. Social relations are important to cavy community living, too.

Cavies like to live in small groups and will develop a hierarchy (or pecking order) in the group. Among adult boars, one is usually the dominant animal. This "alpha" male will be bossy toward other boars and not allow them to mate with any sows. Males may fight with each other, especially if they are housed with females. Fights over sows can be serious and in some cases end in death. However, if the cage is large enough, boars may simply try to avoid each other after an aggressive encounter.

Females are usually subordinate to the dominant male, in other words, they rank below him and will not challenge him. However, they will form a pecking order among themselves, although this hierarchy is not as strictly enforced as the one among the boars. A castrated male often finds himself at the bottom of the pecking order, with females taking food away from him.

Cavies mark their territory with anal and sebaceous gland secretions and urine. The pecking order is maintained through scent-marking, vocalizations, threat displays, and, rarely, fights. Boars will not fight with sows.

Baby cavies have the best of all worlds. They follow the adults about, whether related or not, and the adults are usually very tolerant of them. When they are not following the adults, they are playing with one another. They get along well together almost all of the time.

When a new individual is introduced to an established group, all cavies tend to come out of hiding to investigate. They cautiously approach, usually in single file, to sniff and nuzzle noses, ears, and anogenital areas to investigate the new arrival. The dominant male may attack the newcomer if it is a male.

Cavies love to congregate and seek out each other's companionship. They crowd close together and eat in groups. They seldom quarrel over food, although they will sometimes sideswipe one another very hard or climb over the top of each other at the food dish. Cavies don't

The Immobility Response

It is possible to cause an immobility response lasting one to ten minutes simply by laying a cavy on its back against a flat surface and pressing gently on its abdomen. This is considered to be a cavy's last-resort effort to avoid capture by predators. This is mentioned for the purpose of interest and information only. Please don't do this to your pet and stress him unnecessarily.

hide their food from each other or store it away. For the most part, cavies are very peaceful individuals that don't mind sharing.

Cavy Behaviors

Like people, cavies have a variety of behaviors and act differently depending on their circumstances. Here are some basic cavy behaviors to help you learn how to interpret your pet's moods and attitudes.

Aggressive behavior: Although cavies are usually mild-mannered and friendly, there are times when they will quarrel among themselves. Arguments are usually between boars in an effort to establish dominance or to claim a sow. Fighting can also take place between noncompatible females. Aggression is accompanied by threatening vocalizations.

Play behavior: Sometimes you will see your cavy run through an entire repertoire of play behavior consisting of jumps, head shaking and hopping, bucking, cavorting, body twisting, and running. Play behavior occurs more often with very young animals and may be a form of early courtship behavior in males. (Courtship and hopping with a shake of the head become associated as males mature.) Play may also be an evolutionary form of "antipredator flight" play, providing a way for cavies, in the days when they were wild, to practice movements that would allow them to escape from predators. Play behavior is seen frequently among littermates.

Curiosity and interest: When your cavy is curious or interested, he will approach cautiously and sniff the air, sometimes lifting a front paw. He may remain on all fours, testing the air, poised to take off at a run if things seem unsafe.

Mating behavior: Males investigate females by chasing them, sniffing at the anogenital area, and purring. Sows in estrus flatten their backs, raise their hindquarters, and stand with the hind feet apart.

Fear: A cavy responds to fear by "freeze or flight." This means that it will either freeze in place, or bolt and run away as fast as it can. It is easy to tell when your cavy is startled. If he can, he will race back to his nest box or hiding place immediately. This type of wild runaway behavior

is called "scattering." If you startle a group of cavies, they will panic and scatter randomly in all directions. Often, this results in accidents and injuries. However, sometimes, if your cavy is very frightened, he will freeze and remain in place, for several seconds or several minutes. In some cases your pet may remain "frozen" for up to 20 minutes.

• Your cavy will usually run if he sees a sudden or unexpected movement. There is no organization to the way cavies flee. If they are together in a group and are startled, they all run off in different directions. By scattering, they make it more difficult for a predator to catch them.

• Your cavy will "freeze," rather than run, if he hears a loud, sudden, or unfamiliar noise. In technical terms, this is called an "immobility response." Your pet may arch his head up with the eyes wide open (with an almost "bug-eyed" expression) and the front legs extended. Sometimes this position can be maintained for as long as 20 minutes. By not moving, a cavy lessens the chances that a predator will find or chase it. A frightened cavy is not aggressive and is not likely to attack. However, if your pet is startled, allow him time to calm down before you try to pick him up because in his fear he may try to bite you when you handle him.

Cavy Communication

Cavies rely on their senses of sight, hearing, smell, and touch to communicate with one another, recognize their owners, identify other animals, and avoid predators.

Cavies communicate in many ways:
• Body language, or visual cues.
• Sense of touch, or tactile communication.
• Sense of smell and olfactory signals.
• Voice signals, or vocalizations.

Body Language

Baby cavies' eyes are open at birth, but it isn't until they are around 25 days of age that their depth perception and ability to discriminate objects is significantly improved. Perhaps that's why they follow

adults around so much during the first few weeks of life.

How well can a cavy see? Well enough to observe, respond, and communicate to each other through body language, a method of expressing moods and intentions by posturing.

Your pet's body language is easy to recognize. Once you learn to interpret it, you will have no problem knowing when your pet is happy, feels threatened, is acting aggressively, is displaying mating behavior, or is playing.

Tactile and Olfactory Communication (Senses of Touch and Smell)

Tactile

Close contact: Cavies love to crowd together. They actively seek each other's company and contact. They enjoy resting their chin or forepaws and chest on each other and sometimes they huddle together parallel, with their noses facing in the same, or opposite, directions. This close body contact may be a way to exchange olfactory information and individual identification. It is also likely that the animals derive comfort and a sense of security by being together. Baby cavies will sometimes sit on top of their mother. By crowding together, cavies with established friendly relationships keep each other company and share warmth and the same body scents.

Cavy Body Language

	Behavior	Situation	Meaning	Function
Relaxed	Resting, eyes usually open, stretched out, lying down	Usually resting in home cage or familiar area	Comfortable in environment, safe, and secure	Resting
Offensive stance	Head raised, mouth open, forelegs extended, hindquarters crouched (accompanied by pilo-erection and tooth chattering), head thrusting and running at opponent	Offensive encounter with another animal	Aggression	Prelude to a fight; attempts to frighten opponent away
Swaying walk	Sways hips from side to side while walking, accompanied by tooth chattering, purring, and circling	Male aggression toward another male, or female's receptivity to breeding	Aggression or breeding behavior	Displays dominance or receptivity
Hair raising (pilo-erection)	Normally the fur lies flat against the body. Pilo-erection causes the hair to stand up from the skin, usually around the shoulders	Alarmed, encounter with another animal; aggressive encounter between males	Threat	Frightens opponent, appears larger, intimidates
Lordosis	Flattened back, raised hindquarters with hind feet placed apart	Female in estrus encounter with male, submissive posture	Receptive sexual behavior; can also be submissive posture	Permits breeding, or if used as a submissive posture, intended to ward off attack
Nose pointing (up)	Pointing the nose up and sometimes away	Submissive posture	Defensive position, or male's response to rebuff from female	Submission; wards off attack from a dominant male
Hops, chasing, body twisting, running	Play	Friendly encounter	Friendly, social interactions, especially among young cavies	Play, possibly to practice movements necessary to escape predators
Circling	Males threaten each other by circling, or a male pursues a female by circling her	Aggression or mating behavior	Aggression	Dominates the other animal in the area
Freezes (immobility response)	"Freezes" in place, eyes bulging, forelegs extended, neck arched	Response to loud, sudden, unfamiliar sounds	Frightened	Avoids detection by predators or unable to move

Olfactory

Scent-marking with urine: Urine is used as a form of communication among cavies, although we're not sure in what capacity. Females that are not receptive to a persistent male's breeding attempts may raise their hindquarters and urinate. While the boar is occupied with the new scent and substance, the sow will escape.

Males also urinate on unreceptive females. As the boar skips past the sow he will throw his leg over her and spray urine. This behavior is called "enurination." It is thought to be the boar's method of identifying the sow, by scent-marking her as a member of his group. As rude as it seems, it is not unique to cavies. Other rodent species exhibit similar behavior.

Scent-marking with scent glands: Cavies have many sebaceous glands along the back and around the anus. The scent glands located in folds around the anal and genital region are important for scent-marking. If you see your cavies sliding their rumps from side to side, or pressing them against objects, or squatting and dragging their bottoms along the ground, they are marking their territory. These behaviors are seen most often after urination, or when they are in new surroundings, or during mating encounters. (Sometimes the anal folds in males must be

Cavy Urine

Cavy urine is opaque and creamy yellow in color. It contains ammonium phosphate crystals and calcium carbonate. The urine can form calcified scales on cage pans, so be sure to put enough litter in the litter pan and change it frequently to reduce odors.

cleaned, especially in older animals, to reduce odors. The scent glands on the rump can also get a little "gummy" and need to be cleaned as needed with a gentle shampoo.)

Vocalization (Voice Signals)

Cavies have keen hearing. In fact, they are very sensitive to loud noises and are easily frightened by them. They can hear sounds ranging from 500 to the ultrasonic range as high as 50,000 Hz.

Cavies produce a variety of sounds that signal their moods. Researchers have measured, recorded, and categorized the sounds according to duration and frequency. The following is a description of a few of the main sounds you will learn to recognize when your cavy communicates.

Squeal: The squeal is a long, loud, high-pitched noise. You will have no doubt about this sound when you hear it, but let's hope that you never do. It is the sound a cavy makes when it

Cavy Vocalizations

Sound	Activity
Chirp	Warning or distress call
Chutt	Exploration, normal activity
Chutter (often followed by a whine)	Distress, discomfort
Low churr or purr	Contentment when being petted; can be aggressive in presence of other cavies; also sound made by male in presence of female in estrus
Growl	Threat, fear
Grunt	Sound made by dominant male to subordinate males, threatening to attack
Purring	Aggressive sound made by males that are about to fight with each other
Scream	Fear, cornered, losing a fight
Squeal	Response to pain or injury
Tooth chatter	Can be contentment (while being petted), or fear or threat, conflict, depending on circumstances
Tweet	Mother's sound when cleaning babies
Whine	Defense, trying to evade or avoid a situation
Whistle	Call usually made to owner; a greeting upon arrival; a demand for attention

is injured and in pain. If your pet ever makes this sound, take him to your veterinarian immediately to determine the cause and find him some relief.

Growl: Cavies don't growl often, but the sound is easy to recognize. It is a deep, guttural sound. A cavy may growl if it is cornered or feels threatened. It indicates aggression and is often accompanied by tooth chattering.

Tooth chatter: Cavies that chatter their teeth are frightened, agitated, or angry, and may bite or fight. They should be approached with caution and not handled until they have had time to calm down. Some cavies will chatter their teeth when they are being petted and this is a sign of satisfaction, not anger.

Chirp: Chirps are low-intensity sounds that your pet may make when he is distressed or upset.

Chutt: This sounds just as it's spelled. You will hear this sound during your pet's normal activities and while he investigates his cage. It is a very brief sound.

Chutter: This is a long, quavering sound that rises and falls. You will hear it when your pet is fearful or tries to run from something or when he is distressed.

Scream: If your cavy screams, he is extremely upset and also very frightened. He is in a situation from which he thinks he cannot escape, such as a losing battle or being pushed into a corner. Your pet is as terrified as he sounds and needs to be rescued.

Whistle: This is an unmistakable sound that you will hear often. It is the sound your pet will make whenever he wants attention from you or calls to you. You'll probably hear this sound every time you come home or when you open the refrigerator door.

Whine: Cavies whine when they want to avoid a situation or protect themselves.

Hair Pulling

Sometimes cavies pull each other's hair out in mouthfuls and eat it. This type of behavior is usually seen in overcrowded conditions or stressful environments. It can become serious and develop into a form of aggression, with subordinate animals suffering the most.

Hair pulling (sometimes called "barbering") can progress to aggressive nibbling and eventual cannibalism of the ears. If you see any of your cavies pulling on each other's hair or nibbling one another in an unfriendly manner—remember: Mutual grooming doesn't take place among cavies—remove the subordinate animals or give your pets more space. You can easily identify your "underdogs." They are the ones with bald spots, areas of thinning hair, patches of hair missing, or in the worst cases, parts of their ears missing. The dominant animals usually have no signs of hair loss.

Some cavies pull hair to be bossy and have their own way. You may see some of your pets pull at each other's hair to butt in front at the water bottle or feeder. Baby cavies may pull hair from their mother. This usually occurs at end of lactation and may also be a sign of aggression toward the mother, who may not be producing as much milk as the pups would like.

When hair is pulled, it is usually also ingested (eaten) and if hair pulling is excessive or becomes a habit, hair balls can form in your pet's digestive tract and cause an obstruction.

Your Cavy's Elimination Behaviors

Cavies have some elimination behaviors that may seem very strange to most of us, but are perfectly normal for cavies. It's helpful to understand these behaviors because they have a lot to do with successful housetraining.

When a cavy urinates it often backs up, sometimes into a corner, and quivers its rump. Cavies often pick an area of the cage, usually a corner, where they prefer to urinate. Unfortunately, they are not as careful about defecating and let fecal pellets drop randomly about the cage whenever they need to eliminate.

If it seems that your pet is constantly dropping pellets wherever he goes, that's because he is. A cavy spends a lot of his time eating. Although his entire intestinal tract, from his mouth to the very end, is more than 7.5 feet long (2.3 m), it takes only two hours for the animal's stomach to empty his contents into the intestinal tract. From there he requires another eight to thirty hours (average twenty hours) for the food to travel down the intestine and exit in pelleted waste form.

Coprophagy

Coprophagy is the act of eating feces. Cavy stools consist of hard, dry pellets and also soft, moist pellets. The moist pellets contain recyclable nutrients and B vitamins. Cavies raise their hindquarters slightly when they defecate. But when a cavy performs coprophagy (approximately 200 times a day!), it bends forward from a sitting position to take the soft fecal pellet into its mouth as it is passed. This is perfectly normal behavior. In fact, if cavies are prevented from eating their droppings, they will lose weight and digest less fiber.

Pregnant cavies sometimes have difficulty bending over because they are so big and round, so they turn around to find the soft pellets and eat them off the floor of the cage.

Housetraining Your Cavy

Some cavies learn to use a litter box for their toilet, just like a cat or a ferret. It's not difficult to teach your pet to use a litter box, but it does require a lot of time, effort, and patience. Young cavies and adult females are better at learning how to use a litter box than males are. Not all cavies are clever enough to be housetrained.

1. It's easiest to start with a young cavy. Find a leak-proof box that is easy to clean. Ideally the litter box should be made of metal. If you use a plastic box, remember that your cavy will chew on it. Don't use cardboard. Cavies urinate large quantities of concentrated urine and cardboard will leak and disintegrate.

2. Cover the floor of the litter box with shredded paper or paper pellet litter (avoid scented litter, clay, or clumping litter). Cover the litter with a little bit of straw. This will keep your pet from getting dirty from the litter underneath as it becomes moistened and soiled and crumbles. It will also make the litter box seem more attractive to your cavy so he will be more likely to go into it and explore.

3. Collect some of your pet's recent fecal pellets and scatter them in the box. This is how you show your cavy where he should eliminate. By finding fecal pellets already in place, he will (hopefully) catch on to the idea faster.

Note: Cavies are usually selective about where they eliminate. This sounds silly, after discussing how often they eliminate in food and water dishes, but the fact is, that even if they soil their dishes, most cavies keep their nest box and sleeping areas clean. For the most part, cavies prefer to defecate and urinate in a selected area of the cage. This is usually a corner.

4. Take advantage of your pet's habits. Place the litter box in the

corner of the cage where elimination usually takes place. It may take several days, maybe weeks, before your cavy ventures into the litter pan to investigate. If you happen to be there to see your pet eliminate in the litter pan, reward him immediately with a small treat. If all goes well, he will eventually make an association between eliminating in the litter pan and receiving a food reward.

5. Once your cavy has started to use the litter box regularly, you can relocate the box when your cavy goes outside of the cage to play. For example, if you want to eventually allow your cavy more space in the house, you can start housetraining it by placing the litter box in a small enclosure along with your cavy. Don't try this, however, until

Housetraining Tips

- Be consistent. Select one spot for the litter box and keep it there.
- Be patient. Not all cavies can be trained to a litter box. It may take several weeks before your pet uses the pan reliably.
- Give food rewards. The instant your pet uses the box, reward him with a small food treat.
- Start small. If your pet stops using the litter box, he may not know where it is. Reduce the play area so it is easier to find the pan and start over.
- Do not use scented, clay, or clumping litter.
- Never punish your pet.

your cavy is already using the litter box when he's in the cage.

6. With time, you can increase the area that your cavy can wander, as long as he knows where the litter box is. If your pet has an accident, his range of exploration is probably too large and he doesn't remember where the box is or can't find his way back to the box. It's time to reduce the play area and start training lessons again.

Discipline

Don't be discouraged if your cavy never learns how to use the litter box; some cavies just don't get it. No matter what, *never* scold your cavy and *never* hit him. Cavies cannot be disciplined and such cruel actions would only confuse your pet and make him fearful of you. Your cavy would never make the association between your displeasure and disciplinary action and his normal bodily functions. After all, it's natural for a cavy to eliminate any time, any place, whenever there is the need. If you can train your little friend to use a litter pan, even part of the time, that's quite an accomplishment!

Cavy Charisma

What is it about cavies that make them so irresistibly charming and charismatic? Perhaps it's the way they always seem to be awake and ready to visit when we are, no matter what time it is. Maybe it's their quiet, calm, collected manner. Or maybe it's just their "stay-at-home" nature. All of these attributes add to the cavy's charisma, but did you know there are some interesting biological facts about these qualities we love?

Seldom Sleeping

Think hard for a moment. When was the last time you saw your cavy sleeping? Not napping with its eyes open, but *sleeping*?

Studies have shown that cavies are active most of the time. They are seldom still for more than ten minutes (usually less than six minutes) at a time. They spend most of their time awake (about 20 hours totally each day) and during the time they are awake, more than half of that time is spent in an alert state. Researchers have learned that cavies spend only 4 percent of their day sleeping and that their sleep periods are not longer than six minutes at a time! In fact, sleep periods usually range from 20 seconds to three minutes. In short, in a 24-hour period, cavies are active for more than 20 of those hours. How do they do it? It makes one tired just to think about it.

Homebody at Heart

Cavies like familiar settings and environments. They are comfortable in areas they know and with animals and people they recognize. They spend most of their time in a shelter or hideaway, or lying in contact under, over, or alongside their companions. When they are not active, cavies feel comfortable huddling in groups next to a wall and seldom venture to the center of their cage. Relocating to new surroundings can be very stressful for a cavy.

When moved to a new area, a cavy will hold its body low, as if trying not to fall, while taking slow, cautious steps as it investigates its new surroundings. This could take a while.

If you move your cavies to a larger enclosure, don't expect them to explore and frolic in it the same day—or even the same week. Cavies like to stay put in an area they know and where they feel secure. They are not explorers. Studies showed that one group of cavies took two months to get around to exploring the entirety of an enclosure approximately 45 feet $\times$ 45 feet (15 m $\times$ 15 m).

Young cavies are more adventurous and adapt more quickly to unknown territories than adults. If you want your pets to have a large pen, buy it for them while they are young so you won't upset them with a change later in life.

Calm Surface

Do you think your pet is a little too easygoing, or doesn't seem to care what's going on most of the time? Do you think your pet might not even *know* what's going on? Cavy owners sometimes say that when it comes to cavies, it often seems like the lights are on, but no one's home. Don't let that calm, collected demeanor fool you. A cavy's lack of response to something doesn't mean it isn't processing the information and reacting to it *on the inside*.

Studies have shown that simple activities, such as opening a cage door, or placing an unknown object in the cage, can cause an increase in a cavy's heart rate. We're not completely sure what this means, but whether your pet seems excited or not, your activities are being noticed and are enough to make his little heart pick up a beat.

Chapter Eight
Cavy Health Care

The most important health care you can provide your cavy is preventive health care. Preventing problems is much easier than treating problems. Cavies are fairly hardy animals and with good care your pet should stay healthy into her old age. But if she becomes ill, she will need immediate attention. Without care, a sick cavy can quickly weaken and die.

Keeping Your Cavy Healthy

Essentials of Good Cavy Care
• Good, nutritious food and fresh water
• Plenty of space to run and play
• Clean, dry, draft-free housing
• Comfortable temperature and humidity
• Quiet environment
• Hideaways and nest boxes
• Chew toys to keep teeth healthy
• Interesting toys
• Another cavy to keep her company
• Lots of attention from you

How to Tell If Your Cavy Is Healthy

Sometimes even the best-cared-for animals become ill. Successful recovery depends upon the type of illness and how early the illness was noticed and treated. To recognize a sick cavy, you must first know how a healthy cavy looks and acts. If your pet is acting sluggish, has a dull coat, is hunched up in an abnormal posture, or is not eating or drinking, then there is definitely a problem. The sooner you have the problem diagnosed and begin treatment, the better your pet's chances of recovery.

The table on page 94 lists some ways to tell if your cavy is healthy or not.

If Your Cavy Is Sick

1. The first thing you should do, the moment that you notice your pet is ill, is separate her from any other pets you have. This way, if the problem is contagious, you have reduced the chances of spreading disease to your other animals. Isolating your

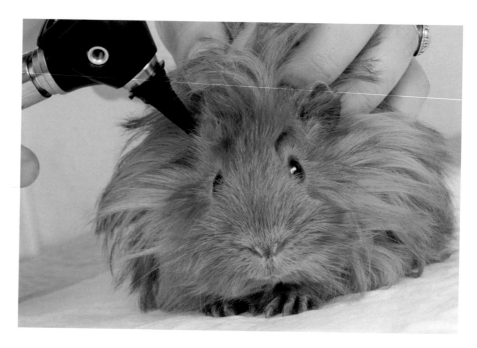

sick cavy gives her a chance to begin her recuperation in peace and quiet without distraction and stress.

2. Contact your veterinarian immediately for advice. An examination is important to diagnose the problem. It is the only way to know exactly what the problem is and if it is contagious to you or your other pets. Your cavy may need to have radio-graphs (X-rays) to check for common problems, such as dental disorders, gastrointestinal disease, and bladder stones. Your cavy may need to be sedated or anesthetized for some procedures or need to have blood collected to run diagnostic tests. A prescription may be given to ensure your pet's survival. Veterinarians are required to personally examine an

Ways to Tell If Your Cavy Is Healthy

	Healthy	Sick
Appearance	Bright, clear eyes, shiny coat, robust, compact	Dull expression, coat in poor condition, patches of hair loss, thin
Behavior	Alert, good appetite, drinking, vocalizing, social, playing, normal urination and defecation	Lethargic, depressed, lack of appetite, not drinking, abnormal elimination, hunched-up position

Physical Characteristics

Lifespan	4 to 8 years
Weight	Boars: 2.1 to 2.6 pounds (950 to 1,200 g)
	Sows: 1.5 to 1.8 pounds (700 to 850 g)
Body temperature	101.5 to 103°F (37.2 to 39.5°C)
Heart rate	230 to 380 beats per minute
Respiration	45 to 100 breaths per minute
Gastrointestinal transit time	8 to 30 hours
Number of chromosomes	64

animal before they can perform any procedures on her or write a prescription for her. They cannot make a diagnosis over the phone.

3. To minimize stress for your cavy while you are transporting her to the veterinary hospital, place her hideaway house or nest box inside of her travel cage and cover the travel cage with a large towel to reduce sounds and light that might startle or disturb your small companion.

4. Continue to keep a close watch on your other cavies and separate out any others that may also become ill.

5. Thoroughly wash all housing, toys, dishes, and bottles that were in contact with your sick pet.

6. Check your pet's food for signs of mold and bad odors. Discard old food and used bedding and nesting material.

7. Check the label on your pet's food to see if there have been changes in ingredients made by the manufacturer.

8. Thoroughly wash your hands after handling any sick animal and before handling other pets or food. This will help prevent the possible spread of contagious disease.

Helping Your Veterinarian Help You

Ideally, you have already selected a veterinarian before the need has arisen. If not, this is a good time to refer to Selecting a Veterinarian (Chapter Six) so you can find someone excellent who is very knowledgeable about cavies and highly skilled in making diagnoses and performing procedures on them.

Make a list of all the questions you want to ask your veterinarian. Your veterinarian will also ask *you* some questions to help make a diagnosis and determine an appropriate treatment. Don't worry if you don't have all the answers; every piece of information will be helpful for your pet.

Before your appointment, make a list of the following information:

- How old is your cavy?
- How long have you owned your pet?
- When did you first notice the problem?
- Does your pet appear to be in any discomfort or pain?
- What, if anything, have you given or done to treat the problem?
- When did your cavy last eat or drink?
- Has there been a change in your pet's diet or living environment? (Take a sample of the food you are feeding your cavy, along with the milling and ingredients information from the food container, to your veterinarian.)
- When did your cavy last have a bowel movement?
- Does your cavy have normal stools, or constipation, or diarrhea?
- Are there any staining or caked feces around the anus or perineum?
- Is your pet drooling and unable to chew?
- Are there any other animals at home? If so, what kind and how many?
- How many animals are housed in the same cage with your sick cavy?
- If you have any other pets, did you purchase any of them recently?
- Do any of your other pets have any problems that seem similar or related?
- What, and how much, do you feed your cavy (including special treats)?
- How is your cavy housed?
- What is the cage-cleaning schedule? (Make sure the soap and sani-tizing products are completely rinsed off the dishes and cage. Tell your veterinarian which cleaning products you are using.)
- Has your pet been exposed to any sick animals or chemicals?
- Where did you obtain your pet?
- If your cavy is a female, is she pregnant? Has she ever had a litter? At what age did she have her first litter? When did she produce her last litter? Did she have any problems with her last pregnancy?
- Add any other findings or relevant information.

Health Problems

Cavies can contract a variety of bacterial and fungal infections and relatively few viral infections. They may be troubled by external (skin, hair, ears) parasites and a few inter-

Medication

- Never give your cavy any medication that was not specifically prescribed for her.
- Cavies are extremely sensitive to many medications. Some common medicines can kill your pet, even in tiny doses, including many antibiotics. Your veterinarian's expertise is absolutely necessary.
- If your cavy is sick or stressed, supplement her with 50 to 100 mg vitamin C daily.

nal (intestinal) parasites. They may also suffer from noncontagious medical conditions, such as dental malocclusion, obesity, diabetes, and genetic disorders. Cancer is relatively rare in cavies less than four to five years of age, except for some types of skin tumors and blood cancers.

The following list of possible health problems may seem very long. Don't let this list frighten or discourage you. Cavies are healthy, happy animals when they receive good care and nutrition. However, when a cavy is ill, it becomes very fragile and its health can rapidly deteriorate in a very short time. Use this list to your advantage so you can recognize health problems in your cavy when they occur,

Immediate Emergency Action If Your Cavy Stops Eating

If your cavy stops eating, it will quickly become deficient in vitamin C. Serious symptoms can develop in less than a week and death can occur in three to four weeks. An early sign of vitamin C deficiency is reluctance to eat, or a painful mouth and inability to eat. A cavy with sore mouth, gums, and jaws, or loose teeth, will quickly starve to death.

Contact your veterinarian immediately to obtain a high-calorie food supplement (such as Nutrical) to force-feed your cavy until it starts to eat on its own.

Are Cavies Resistant to Some Cancers?

Scientists don't have all the answers yet, but it appears that Kurloff cells (or Foa Kurloff cells)—which are unique to cavies and their capybara cousins—together with asparaginase (also found in cavy blood) may play an important role in protecting the animal against certain kinds of cancer. Interestingly, Kurloff cells are observed more often in female cavies than in male cavies, and rarely in young cavies. Kurloff cells correlate with estrogen levels and are highest in pregnant females.

provide immediate first aid, and talk to your veterinarian.

Note: If you are unable to give your cavy food or liquids with a syringe, contact your veterinarian immediately. In most cases, aggressive medical therapy is necessary, including vitamin C injection, fluid therapy, and, in very serious cases, passing a nasogastric tube directly into the stomach to prevent starvation and death.

Bite Wounds

Cavies are mild-mannered and nonaggressive. Although during a confrontation they may chatter their teeth, rumble, and shriek, they rarely bite one another (boars housed together with a sow are the exceptions). You can reduce the incidence of bite wounds by making sure your animals are not overcrowded and that they are compatible. Do not house boars together unless they have been raised together peacefully since birth and there are no sows housed with them.

Because cavies have such long, sharp teeth, bite wounds can be serious injuries. Deep puncture wounds frequently become infected and form abscesses.

To check your cavy for bite wounds, push the fur back with your fingers and look for any lumps, bumps, puncture holes, swelling, redness, tenderness, or pus. If a bite wound is deep, it can cause muscle and nerve damage.

Treatment: Clean the wound with a mild antiseptic solution. Keep the wound clean and allow it to drain until it has closed on its own and healed. Consult your veterinarian.

Dehydration

Dehydration occurs when an animal loses too much water from the body. There are many causes of dehydration, including not drinking enough water, illness and diarrhea, and exposure to a hot, dry environment.

Treatment: The treatment for dehydration is rehydration, which is replenishing the body with water. When an animal becomes dehydrated, it also loses minerals from her body. If your pet is dehydrated, give her immediate access to fresh drinking water. Do not try to force

Emergency Liquid Vitamin C Formula

To start first aid emergency supplementation:

- Crush one 250 mg vitamin C tablet.
- Add ⅟₁₅ ounce (2 ml) fresh orange juice.
- Add ⅟₁₅ ounce (2 ml) fresh water.
- Mix juice, water, and vitamin C powder together well.
- Place the tip of the syringe (without a needle) at the side of your pet's mouth.
- Feed liquid slowly, drop by drop, allowing your pet time to swallow.
- Make sure your cavy does not aspirate fluid into her lungs.
- Contact your veterinarian immediately.

water on your pet if she is unconscious or too weak to drink on her own, because she may aspirate the water into her lungs. Contact your veterinarian immediately and ask if a balanced electrolyte solution (a mixture of water and necessary minerals in the proper dilution for rehydration) is advised. Electrolyte solutions are available from your veterinarian. In an emergency, you can also find electro-

How Much Water Should You Give Your Dehydrated Cavy?

If your pet is dehydrated, give her 3 to 4 ounces (100 ml) of water per 2 pounds (kg) of body weight per day until she is drinking normally on her own.

Emergency Feeding Formula

- Blend baby food mixed vegetables (use only baby foods that *do not* contain onions) or guinea pig pellets or a combination of both with enough water to make the mixture a consistency thin enough to feed with a syringe (without a needle!).
- Add one crushed vitamin C tablet (250 mg) to the mixture daily.
- Prepare the mixture immediately before feeding.
- Feed mixture slowly to prevent aspiration.

If your cavy refuses the mixture, try offering a soy-based liquid formula.

This formula is provided only for use short term, in an emergency. Your veterinarian can provide you with a more balanced commercial hand-feeding formula to keep on hand at all times in case of an emergency, such as Critical Care (Oxbow Hay Co.).

lyte solutions formulated for human babies (such as Pedialyte) available at pharmacies and supermarkets. Keep a bottle on hand in case of emergency.

Warning: Do not give your pet homemade salt or sugar mixtures without consulting your veterinarian. In the wrong proportions, these will do more harm than good and further dehydrate your pet.

Dental Problems

Cavy teeth, incisors and molars, are open-rooted and grow throughout life. The outer surface of the incisors is harder than the inside material, so as your cavy chews, her teeth are constantly chiseled and sharpened. There are no nerves in the incisors, except at the base of the tooth where growth takes place.

Check your cavy regularly for dental problems. It is not easy to thoroughly examine a cavy's mouth or all of her teeth. Cavies have narrow mouths and large tongues, and your cavy will squeal and struggle if you try to exam her mouth. This is a job for your veterinarian, who has special equipment and medications designed for this purpose. If your cavy is drooling, having difficulty eating, or refuses to eat, she likely has a painful mouth. Ask your veterinarian to examine her mouth right away so she doesn't suffer, lose weight, and weaken.

Most dental problems can be avoided by providing safe chew toys, a balanced diet, and by removing animals with dental problems from the breeding program.

Malocclusion: When the incisors or molars do not grow in proper alignment, the teeth wear unevenly. This is called "malocclusion." One or more of the misdirected teeth may grow into the delicate tissues of the mouth. The molars can overgrow laterally, injuring the tongue or inside of the cheeks. This painful condition makes it difficult or impossible for the animal to eat.

Malocclusion of the cheek teeth often causes drooling and refusal to eat. It is difficult for you to detect simply by looking because a cavy's mouth is small and it's hard to see inside to examine. This is a job for your veterinarian. It requires special equipment and anesthesia to get a good look inside and to correct the problem; filing the molars or premolars may be necessary on a regular basis. If the problem isn't treated, your pet could slowly starve to death.

Malocclusion is often an inherited problem, but it can also be caused by trauma or infection. Poor diet and vitamin C deficiency may also play a role.

Signs of malocclusion include protruding teeth, loss of appetite, weight loss, drooling, inability to swallow, a swollen, painful mouth, "slobbers," and "lumps."

Treatment: The offending teeth will need to be trimmed or filed back. The teeth will grow back and need to be trimmed regularly throughout the animal's life. Many cases of incisor malocclusions are linked to problems with the molars. In some cases, the tongue can be trapped and injured by the molars. Do not try to trim your pet's teeth yourself. You may be accidentally bitten, and you can break the teeth or cause pain and permanent tooth loss. Incisor and molar trimming or shaping should only be done by your veterinarian, who will use a high-speed dental drill or other similar specialized equipment.

The teeth will grow back and need to be trimmed regularly.

Note: Malocclusion is often inherited. Cavies that have malocclusion should not be used in the breeding program.

"Slobbers": "Slobbers" is drooling due to excessive salivation, inability to swallow, or pain. It is often associated with malocclusion of the cheek teeth and accompanied by weight loss, gradual wasting, and eventually death from starvation.

"Lumps": "Lumps" is also known as cervical lymphadenitis. It is a common disease in cavies caused by a bacterial infection due to *Streptococcus zooepidemicus,* and sometimes *Streptobacillus moniliformis*. When the mouth is damaged by malocclusion or sharp objects (such as hay stems), bacteria invade the tissues and multiply. As the bacteria multiply, abscesses form in the lymph nodes. When a cavy has lumps, it looks like it has the mumps. The abscesses may rupture and reform repeatedly. The germs spread from the lymph nodes throughout the body and cause serious problems, even death.

Treatment: Treatment for lumps is surgical correction and appropriate antibiotics. If surgery is not possible, rinsing and draining the abscesses and medicating may be successful treatment in some cases.

Remember to wear protective gloves when you are cleaning or rinsing the abscesses. (Vinyl gloves are recommended because some people are allergic to latex gloves.) Do not allow children to help you with this task.

Broken teeth: Sometimes an incisor will break (often due to trauma). It will grow back, but during that time, the tooth opposite the missing or broken tooth may become overgrown because it has nothing to grind against. To prevent injury to the mouth, the opposite tooth will need to be trimmed by your veterinarian until the broken tooth grows back.

Gum infection and tooth loss: Gums may become infected and a tooth may require removal. Your cavy may have a swollen mouth and refuse to eat. Tend to this problem right away so your pet doesn't go hungry and lose weight. Dental extraction is a job for your veterinarian.

Sore, bleeding, inflamed gums are also signs of vitamin C deficiency.

Ear Problems

Even though your pet's ears are relatively large, it is not always easy to tell if she is having ear problems because it is difficult to see inside the ear canal. Ear problems may be caused by infection, injury, or parasites. Signs include pain, scratching at the ears, head shaking, tilting the head to one side (torticollis), and loss of balance.

Treatment: Place a drop of mineral oil on a cotton-tipped swab and gently wipe away any dirt or debris

from your cavy's ears. This may also give your pet some relief from itching and smother parasites if they are present. Contact your veterinarian immediately if the condition persists or appears painful.

Torticollis and loss of balance may be due to inner ear infection caused by germs spread from the respiratory tract. Appropriate, safe antibiotics are indicated; however, torticollis may not respond to antibiotics, and in some cases the head tilt may be permanent.

Ear problems due to infection or parasites require a veterinary evaluation, cleansing, and treatment with a safe prescription medication for successful results.

Eye Problems

Eye problems may develop from injury, infection, or irritating substances. Check your pet daily to be sure her eyes are clear and bright. If your cavy's eyes are dull, have a discharge, or are closed, place your pet in a dark room and contact your veterinarian. Many eye problems are painful and make the eyes sensitive to light. Your veterinarian can provide a gentle eyewash and eye ointment or drops, if necessary.

Conjunctivitis: Injuries and bacterial infections can cause inflammation of the tissues surrounding the eyes. Treatment with antibiotics and anti-inflammatory drugs may be necessary.

Chlamydophila cavaie causes conjunctivitis, swollen eyelid margins, and tearing in young cavies two to eight weeks of age. The disease can be spread from cavy to cavy and can be carried by some birds. Humans cannot contract the disease from cavies.

Usually the disease will run its course and the animal will recover. However, in cases where pneumonia is also present, death may result. Contact your veterinarian for an appropriate eye ointment.

Cataracts and corneal ulcers: Many eye problems look similar; for example, ulcers of the cornea and cataracts both give the eyes a cloudy appearance. Sharp bedding can injure the eyes and give them a cloudy appearance. If not treated, loss of vision can result.

Some eye problems cannot be treated or may be signs of additional health problems. Cataracts are frequently seen in diabetic animals. Don't feed your pet sugary treats and keep her sugar consumption to a minimum, to help prevent the development of diabetes and cataracts.

Antibiotics

Sensitivity to Antibiotics (antibiotics taken by mouth, injected, or applied topically).
Also called: Antibiotic Toxicity or Antibiotic Associated Enterotoxemia.

- Cavies normally have an established type of bacterial population (gram-positive bacteria) in their intestinal tract. When they are given certain antibiotics to treat an infection, these "good" intestinal bacteria are killed along with the "bad" germs that are being targeted.
- When the gram-positive bacteria die, gram-negative bacteria multiply in the intestinal tract in their place.
- The gram-negative bacteria, such as *Clostridium difficile*, produce toxins.
- The toxins are released and cause diarrhea, hemorrhage, dehydration, drop in body temperature, and loss of appetite.
- Without immediate treatment and supportive care, the cavy quickly dies.

Do not give your cavy any medications prescribed for you or for your other pets. Consult your veterinarian about the safety of any medication before giving it to your cavy.

Treatment: Many eye conditions are very painful and most require veterinary expertise, so make an appointment with your veterinarian immediately. Place your cavy in a dark room until your veterinary appointment.

Some eye conditions can be complicated and may need to be treated by an eye specialist—a veterinary ophthalmologist. For example, some types of cataracts can be removed; however, it is difficult to do this because of the small size of the cavy's eye and the large size of its lens. This is a job for an expert only.

Gastrointestinal Problems

Parasites, bacterial and viral infections, improper diet, stress, or unclean housing conditions all can cause gastrointestinal problems. These problems are often painful conditions and can cause bloat, constipation, or diarrhea.

Bloat: Bloat is the accumulation of gas within the gastrointestinal tract. Gas and fluid accumulate, causing the abdomen to swell and distend. There are a variety of causes of bloat, including foods high in starches and sugars, such as grains and fruits; gastrointestinal stasis; infections; obstructions of the gastrointestinal tract; and gas-producing foods.

Warning: Bloat is an emergency situation. It is extremely painful and can rapidly result in death.

Treatment: Contact your veterinarian immediately. This is an emergency. Treatment depends on the severity and cause.

Constipation: Constipation is difficulty passing dry, hard feces. Causes of constipation include dehydration, insufficient water intake, dry or hot environment, obstruction of the intestinal tract, and parasitism.

Treatment: Be sure your cavy can reach the water bottle and that the sipper tube is working properly. Replace dry food with moist foods until the stools return to normal. Consult your veterinarian.

Diarrhea: Disease (bacterial, viral, or parasitic), infection, stress, or an excess of greens, fruits, and vegetables in the diet can all cause diarrhea (soft, mucous, or liquid stools). The anal area may be wet and soiled.

If not treated quickly, diarrhea can lead to dehydration and possibly death.

Gastrointestinal Parasites

Intestinal Parasite	Symptoms
Protozoa *(Cryptosporidium wrairi)* Spread by ingestion; weanling pups and immunosuppressed animals are most susceptible	Weight loss, diarrhea, and death
Protozoa *(Eimeria cavia* and *Balantidium caviae)* Spread by ingestion; rarely causes symptoms	Diarrhea in some cases from *Eimeria cavia*
Roundworm *(Paraspidodera uncinata)* Spread by ingestion	Seldom causes symptoms

Treatment: If your cavy has diarrhea, she may need medicine to recover. Be careful! Some antibiotics cause severe diarrhea from antibiotic-associated enterotoxemia. Consult your veterinarian.

Rectal stool impaction: Sick and old cavies often suffer from rectal stool impaction. Fecal material accumulates in the rectum. The dry stool around the rectal area blocks the anal opening, and feces (stools) cannot pass.

Treatment: Use a warm washcloth to soak and remove the dried stool and clean it away from the rectal area so your pet can eliminate her stools normally. Ask your veterinarian to prescribe a topical antibiotic ointment that you can apply gently to the area to ease minor skin irritation.

Heatstroke

Cavies overheat easily and are often victims of heatstroke. Be sure that your pet's cage is not in direct sunlight and is not close to a woodstove, fireplace, radiator, or heater. If you must transport your pet, never leave her in the car. On a warm day, a car can heat up to 120°F (48.9°C) in a few minutes, even with the windows partially open. Adequate ventilation is also important to prevent your pet from becoming too hot.

If your cavy is exposed to high temperatures, she will lie down and stretch out flat in an attempt to cool herself. In a short time she will become weak, unresponsive, and eventually comatose. Without immediate emergency treatment she will die. You must quickly and safely drop your pet's temperature and give her fluids to treat dehydration.

Treatment: To cool down your cavy, hold her in your hands in a sink of cool (not cold) water. Be sure to keep her head above water so she can safely breathe. Once your cavy has regained consciousness, dry her gently and place her in a dry, dark, comfortable cage to rest. Next, give

How Much Vitamin C Should You Give Your Sick Cavy Each Day?

Your sick cavy should receive 50 to 100 mg vitamin C supplement every day until her health and condition have improved.

your pet fluids, either water or a balanced electrolyte solution, according to your veterinarian's recommendation. Make sure your pet is fully conscious and able to swallow so that the fluid does not go into the lungs.

Injury and Trauma

Small animals have a way of sometimes being in the wrong place at the wrong time. If your cavy is dropped, stepped on, attacked by the family dog or cat, or injured in any way, try to determine how seriously she is hurt. Dropped cavies often suffer a broken foot, leg, hock, or back. If your pet is dropped, observe her closely to be sure she acts and moves about normally and continues to eat and drink. Isolate your pet in a clean, comfortable cage and do not handle her more than necessary. Contact your veterinarian for advice.

Pododermatitis: Pododermatitis (inflamed, sore feet) is caused by housing cavies on wire mesh floors or sharp, abrasive bedding material. Heavy or overweight animals are most commonly affected, although pododermatitis can occur in cavies of all sizes.

The surfaces of the feet become tender and sore from the pressure of the irritating surface against them. Eventually, the bottoms of the feet ulcerate and become infected. The infection can travel through the tissues and into the bone, causing osteomyelitis, a life-threatening condition.

Pododermatitis is very painful. Affected cavies are reluctant or unable to walk. They cry out in pain and lose weight due to lack of appetite and ongoing infection.

Treatment: Soak the foot to clean it, wrap it in bandages, and give your pet soft bedding. Make sure her environment is clean and dry. Consult your veterinarian for an evaluation. Pododermatitis is a serious condition that can lead to death.

Note: Pododermatitis is sometimes incorrectly called "bumblefoot." Bumblefoot is a foot disease of fowls, not cavies!

Muscle and Skeletal Problems

Scurvy: Vitamin C deficiency has been discussed in detail (see Chapter Five, Feeding Your Cavy). Lack of vitamin C causes serious problems

in collagen production. Collagen is necessary for healthy blood vessels, joints, and gums. Collagen helps keep teeth firmly rooted in place.

Signs of vitamin C deficiency include loose teeth, malocclusion, sore and bleeding gums, enlargements along the ribs (at the costochondral junctions), fractures, loss of appetite, rough hair coat, diarrhea, lameness, increased susceptibility to infections, crying in pain, and death.

Treatment: Supplement the diet with vitamin C in sufficient quantities. Cavies that are going to recover usually show improvement within a few days of starting vitamin C supplementation; however, it may take more than a week for the animal to feel and behave normally.

Vitamin E deficiency: Cavies that do not receive enough vitamin E in their diets will eventually develop muscular dystrophy and die within one week of the onset of symptoms. Signs of insufficient vitamin E intake include hind limb weakness, lameness, or paralysis. Breeding animals become infertile or produce deformed offspring. The problem is diagnosed by symptoms and laboratory tests.

Treatment: 5 mg of vitamin E per pound (10 mg per kg) of body weight.

Nails

Overgrown and misdirected toenails can become caught or snagged on something and tear and bleed.

Unless the nail bed has been damaged, the toenail will grow back. In the meantime, the injury should be kept clean to prevent infection.

Treatment: A torn nail may be trimmed carefully using nail clippers designed for human babies. These small clippers work well for cavy nails. When you trim your pet's torn nail, just trim the very tip of it to prevent bleeding and additional damage.

Neurological Problems

Lymphocytic choriomeningitis virus: This virus is spread in the urine of infected rodents and spread by contact and biting insects. It causes paralysis of the hind limbs and meningitis. Lymphocytic choriomeningitis is a common disease of mice and hamsters, but is rarely seen in pet cavies. The disease is contagious to humans and causes meningitis and flulike symptoms.

There is no treatment.

Reproductive and Urogenital Problems

Sows

Although you might not intend to own a pregnant cavy or raise a baby cavy, it is possible that when you acquired your cavy, she was already pregnant—unknown to you. This is not an unusual situation, although it is an unexpected one that can present a variety of potential problems. We will discuss these problems here so that you will be able to recognize and address them, as many of these problems can be life-threatening for your pet.

Dystocia: It is not unusual for cavies to have difficulty giving birth. If the fetus is too large to pass through the birth canal, it will die while it is still inside the uterus. It may eventually pass and be born dead (stillbirth).

This life-threatening condition is more common with young, immature sows, small sows weighing less than one and one-half pounds (680 g), or old sows. Old sows often have small litters (only one or two pups). Pups from small litters tend to be larger than pups from large litters and have more difficulty passing through the birth canal.

A cavy should not be in labor more than 20 minutes before giving birth or between the births of pups. If your cavy has been in labor for more than 20 minutes, contact your veterinarian immediately!

Dystocia is an emergency situation. Without immediate veterinary care (Caesarean section surgery is required), the pups and mother will die.

Abortion: Abortion is the death and loss of the unborn fetus at any stage in development. There are many causes of abortion in cavies, including
- Vitamin C deficiency (scurvy)
- Age related (too young or too old)
- Bacterial infections (several types, including *Erysipelothrix*, *Salmonella*, and *Streptococcus*)
- Viral infections (*Herpes* virus)
- Ketosis or Pregnancy Toxemia
- Obesity
- Stress
- Fright
- Living with an aggressive boar
- Excessive or rough handling
- Changes in environment

Stillbirths: Stillbirth is when the pups are born dead. They can be completely developed and ready to be born but have died in the uterus before birth. Stillbirths are common in sows that have only one pup in the litter.

Uterine inertia: When the muscles of the uterus no longer will or can contract to push out the pups, this is called "uterine inertia." This condition requires immediate emergency care. Your veterinarian will decide if oxytocin injections may be helpful to stimulate the weak muscles of the uterus to contract. In many cases oxytocin is not effective.

Pregnancy Toxemia (Ketosis): Ketosis is a life-threatening condition seen primarily in obese, pregnant sows or sows that are pregnant for the first time and are carrying a large litter. Ketosis can also occur in sows that have never been pregnant, as well as obese boars. Ketosis is caused by obesity, stress, changes in diet or housing, transporting, or fasting (a cavy will not eat when it is stressed, and this is called "stress induced anorexia").

Ketosis usually occurs in the last two weeks of gestation. In some animals, death occurs suddenly, without warning symptoms. In others, signs of weakness, lack of appetite, salivation, incoordination, convulsions, and coma precede death by three to five days.

In pregnancy toxemia, the fetuses press against the body organs and compress the blood vessels. This results in less blood flow to the uterus, and the uterine tissues and fetuses die. Obese sows in their first or second pregnancy carrying more than two pups are most affected.

Animals suffering from ketosis have unusual acetone-like breath odor and clear urine (normal cavy urine is opaque and cloudy).

Prevention is the best way to deal with this deadly condition, for treatment is rarely successful.

To prevent ketosis:
- Keep your cavies at a reasonable weight
- Do not overfeed your cavies

- Do not change your sow's food
- Do not move your sow or change her environment
- Provide fresh greens
- Prevent stress
- Handle pregnant sows as little as possible during the last third of gestation

Uterine Hemorrhage: The sow's uterus can tear or rupture during prolonged or difficult birth. Signs of uterine hemorrhage include vaginal bleeding and inability to deliver pups.

Eclampsia (hypocalcemia): This life-threatening condition is caused by a calcium deficiency and is usually seen after farrowing (giving birth), when the sow is lactating. It can also occur during pregnancy.

Symptoms include depression and muscle spasms. If emergency treatment (an injection of calcium gluconate) is not given immediately, convulsions and death follow rapidly.

Note: Breeders report eclampsia is seen most often in Satin breeds.

Even if your cavy is not pregnant or lactating, she can suffer from other kinds of problems, such as vaginitis.

Vaginitis: Irritating bedding can cause inflammation and infection of the vagina. Bedding should be changed (use a pelleted paper bedding, *not* wood shavings), and the vaginal area should be cleaned gently with a warm, moist cloth.

Ointments and antibiotics may be necessary.

You can prevent some problems of the reproductive system if your cavy has been spayed (undergone an ovariohysterectomy). In addition to the risks of pregnancy, these problems include:

Mastitis: Irritating bedding and unsanitary conditions can cause inflammation and infection of the mammary glands. Bacteria from the soiled, contaminated environment enter through the teat canals and spread throughout the mammary tissue. In more severe cases, bacteria spread and invade tissues throughout the body.

Mastitis is a very painful condition. It leads to weight loss, fever, lack of appetite, depression, and dehydration. The sow's milk becomes thick and tinged with blood and eventually she may stop producing milk completely and abandon her pups.

Mastitis is a serious medical emergency requiring treatment and antibiotics. Without treatment, death usually occurs within a few days.

Cystic ovaries: Cystic ovaries are common in sows more than three years of age. The animals may show signs of illness or appear normal. They may have patchy areas of missing hair or bald spots on their skin.

Cystic ovaries are diagnosed with the help of ultrasound imaging and can be treated surgically or with hormone therapy. Estrogen compounds in moldy hay may cause the problem in some cases.

Uterine prolapse: Prolapse of the uterus is usually associated with partuition (giving birth).

Uterine cancer: Cancer of the uterus is not uncommon in older sows.

Boars

Scrotal impaction: Boars have a rounded shaped scrotum with a depression in the center. The scrotum is covered with a sticky paste-like substance used for scent marking. When boars drag their testicles along the floor of the cage to scent mark, particles (bedding, dirt, hay) stick to this pasty substance and form a foul-smelling mass in the depression of the scrotum. In some boars this collection of material hardens and causes problems, including infertility and death.

Do not try to pull on the mass. Gently clean the scrotum on a regular basis using a moist cotton swab and some mineral oil.

Balanoposthitis: Pieces of bedding can become lodged inside the prepuce (sheath of the penis) and cause severe irritation, infection, infertility, and prolapse of the penis. The condition is more common in older boars. It can be severe and requires gentle daily cleaning with a damp, moist cloth and, in most cases, an antibiotic ointment. Zinc oxide ointment can be beneficial in case of emergency until you can contact your veterinarian. Use shredded paper or pelleted paper bedding to help prevent the problem, and check your boar frequently.

Many reproductive problems in boars, such as infections and cancer of the testicles and epididymis, can be prevented by having your boar castrated.

Urinary Problems

Urinary calculi (stones): Small stones can form in the urinary bladder or the urethra and obstruct the out-flow of urine. This problem is common in cavies, especially those older than two years of age. Bladder stones are more common in sows and urethral stones are seen more frequently in boars.

Stones can be very painful. Diet, age, and bacterial infections influence the development of stones. There is no known prevention at this time.

Treatment: Surgical removal of stones is necessary if they are preventing urination or causing pain. Unfortunately, stones tend to recur, and more than one surgical procedure is sometimes needed.

Urethral blockage: Blockage of the urethra is usually seen in older boars. The urethra becomes plugged with mucus, pus, and debris, making it impossible to urinate. Some species of bacteria seriously aggravate the condition.

Do not feed foods high in oxalates and substances that cause or contribute to the problem.

Urinary tract infection: Infections of the urinary tract are not uncommon and can be associated with urinary calculi. It is a painful condition that requires immediate veterinary care.

Respiratory Problems

Pneumonia: Pneumonia, especially pneumonia caused by bacterial infection, is the most frequent cause of death in cavies. If you hear your cavy wheezing or sneezing, take these symptoms seriously. Contact your veterinarian immediately. Your pet may have developed an allergy, or fine, powdery bedding may be irritating her respiratory tract. In more serious cases, your cavy may have been exposed to dangerous germs (bacterial or viral), or to a damp, cold, drafty environment. Whatever the initial cause, your pet risks developing pneumonia.

Cavies are very susceptible to respiratory disease caused by bacteria *Bordetella bronchiseptica* and *Streptococcus pneumoniae*. These bacteria can be spread by direct contact or in the air (aerosolized droplets of contaminated material, as produced when sneezing). The germs are spread to cavies from humans, dogs, cats, rabbits, pigs, rats, and birds.

Signs of pneumonia include breathing difficulty, open-mouth breathing, discharge from the eyes and nose, lack of appetite, inactivity, and weight loss. The germs spread though the body, causing tilting of the head when the inner ear is infected and uterine infections and abortions when the reproductive organs are invaded.

Pneumonia is a life-threatening disease. Cavies respond poorly to treatment for pneumonia and the disease usually causes death, especially if it is not treated immediately with the proper medication. Consult your veterinarian.

Lung cancer: Pulmonary adenoma is a common lung tumor of cavies. Symptoms include difficulty breathing, loss of appetite, and wasting.

Treatment: Treatment is limited and there is no cure. Keep your pet as comfortable as possible and consult your veterinarian.

Skin and Hair Problems

Signs of skin problems include loss of fur; sores; dry, flaky, itchy skin; and moist, oozing, reddened skin. Skin problems may be caused by skin parasites (mites, lice, and fleas), allergies, hormonal imbalance, improper diet, stress, disease, or fungal and bacterial infections. Your veterinarian's expertise is necessary to diagnose the exact cause of your pet's condition. Specific prescription medication may be required to treat the problem successfully.

Trichofolliculoma: Trichofolliculoma is the most common type of skin tumor in cavies. It usually appears as small cystic-type bumps or masses over the rump area. The

tumors are benign (harmless) and can be removed surgically.

Unavoidable Problems

Some medical conditions, such as problems with the heart, kidneys, liver, or other internal organs, may go unnoticed. Many problems associated with aging or genetics, such as diabetes or cancer, cannot be prevented. If your pet has a medical problem you cannot treat or cure, you can still provide the best home remedy of all—good food and a safe, comfortable, loving home.

Zoonotic Diseases

Zoonotic diseases are diseases that can be shared between animals and humans. Many species of ani-mals are carriers of certain diseases that do not make them ill, but can make humans very sick. Likewise,

Sensitivity to Medications

• Cavies are very sensitive to many medications.
• Use only medicines prescribed for your cavy by your veterinarian and give no more than the recommended dose.
• Never give your cavy any medicine intended for you or your other pets.
• Do not treat your cavy for parasites with products prescribed for your other pets without first consulting your veterinarian to be sure the products are safe for cavies!

humans can carry germs to which they are resistant, but that can make some animals sick. Some disease organisms cause illness in both humans and animals.

Cavies share some diseases contagious to humans:

1. Lymphocytic choriomeningitis virus (rare in cavies and usually contracted from hamsters).

2. Ringworm, a fungal disease caused by *Trichophyton mentagrophytes.*

3. Sarcoptid mite, *Trixacarus caviae,* an external parasite.

If your cavy becomes ill, your veterinarian can answer questions you may have about the contagion of different diseases or parasites.

When Surgery Is Necessary

Sometimes surgery is the best, or only, option available to treat your pet's medical problem. In this case, make sure that you have chosen a veterinarian who is experienced and skilled in caring for cavy patients.

Here's a list of common cavy health conditions that are best treated surgically:
• Cervical lymphadenitis ("lumps")
• Uterine infection (pyometra)
• Uterine torsion (twisted uterus)
• Dystocia (difficulty delivering pups through the birth canal)
• Mammary neoplasia (breast cancer)
• Urinary calculi (stones in the urinary bladder)

• Skin tumors
• Tumors of the reproductive organs

Should Your Cavy Be Neutered?

Neutering refers to the removal of some, or all, of the tissues in the body associated with reproduction (testicles in the male, ovaries and uterus in the female). Neutering in the cavy is accomplished surgically.

Neutering your cavy offers many behavioral and health benefits. For example, if you have a boar and a sow and want to house them together but do not want to be continually finding homes for their many offspring, then neutering is a good alternative.

Neutered boars maintain breeding and territorial behaviors if they are neutered after eight months of age. In other words, the boar will continue to pursue and mate with sows (however, the mating will not produce offspring because neutering renders the boar infertile) and will continue to fight with other males. If you have two boars housed together and they dislike each other and fight, neutering will not change their established behavior and personality conflicts.

Boars that are neutered before the age of three months will not grow to be as large as boars that are intact (not neutered). Considering the fact that male cavies reach sexual maturity at around nine to ten weeks of age, the age to neuter a boar housed with sows is just before it reaches puberty. If you have young compatible boars housed together peacefully *without* sows, they probably will not need to be neutered. However, if you decide to have them castrated, you can wait until they are 12 weeks of age so that they can reach their full growth potential.

Risks

Castration is a less invasive procedure than a spay, is easier to perform, and requires less surgical time and, therefore, less anesthesia time. For these reasons, recovery from castration is usually more rapid, and the fee for a castration can be less than the fee for a spay. This doesn't mean that castrating a cavy is easy. It requires a skilled surgeon familiar with cavy anatomy.

Sows recognize castrated boars, perhaps because they no longer smell quite the same to them. Whatever the reasons, some sows will take advantage of the situation. Instead of remaining subordinate to the male, some females will become bossy toward castrated males and dominate them and even take their food away from them. You should keep your pets' relationships and interactions in mind when you make your decision about whether castration or spay is appropriate for your cavies and, if so, which individuals to select for the procedures.

Sometimes neutering is a necessary treatment for a health problem, such as the removal of infected, inflamed, or cancerous reproductive organs. Spaying and neutering can offer health benefits for your pets by preventing pregnancy and reproductive problems such as infection, cysts, and cancer of the reproductive organs.

Advantages

• Eliminate the possibility of developing cancer cysts or infections in the reproductive organs by removing them.
• Reduce fighting, especially among boars.
• Prevent unwanted pregnancies.

Disadvantages

• Cavies can be easily stressed by excessive restraint, transport, or hospitalization.
• Some cavies do not tolerate anesthesia or surgical procedures well.
• All surgical and anesthetic procedures involve an element of risk.

Cavy Health Care Guidelines

Health Problem	Symptoms
Bite wounds	Sores, redness, swelling, infection, pain or tenderness, draining pus
Bloat	Distended abdomen (gastric dilatation), filled with gas and fluid, extreme pain, lack of appetite, inactivity, difficulty breathing, rapid heart rate
Broken teeth	Tooth opposite broken tooth overgrows and damages mouth, causing pain and inability to eat
Cancer	Sick, no appetite, weight loss, depression, inactivity; sometimes visible lumps
Cataracts	Cataracts (cloudy lens)
Constipation and rectal stool impaction	Straining or inability to pass hard, dry feces; depression, lethargy, hunched-up position, dry, ruffled fur, distended abdomen
Dehydration	When skin is pulled up it "tents" and is slow to fall back in place; lethargy; weakness
Dental malocclusion	Protruding or misdirected front teeth, overgrown cheek teeth, loss of appetite, inability to eat, drooling, weight loss, painful mouth, "lumps"
Diarrhea	Soft, mucous, or liquid feces, odor, wet around anus, dehydration, poor appetite, weight loss, lethargy, hunched-up position, distended abdomen
Ear problems	Scratching, head shaking, loss of balance, head tilted to one side, pain
Eye problems	Discharge (runny eyes), or cloudy, dull eyes

Causes	What to Do
Fighting among incompatible animals; overcrowding	Cleanse wounds and allow to drain.
Dietary problems, usually caused by overfeeding foods high in starches and sugars; gastrointestinal stasis; can be caused by environmental stress, or bacterial infections	Life-threatening emergency; contact veterinarian immediately.
Trauma	Have your veterinarian trim tooth opposite broken tooth until damaged tooth grows and all teeth mesh properly.
Old age, viral disease; some cancers are possibly inherited. A common benign skin cancer is trichofolliculoma, usually found over the rump area (can be found in young animals).	Keep pet comfortable; seek veterinary help to treat symptoms. Trichofolliculoma can be removed surgically.
Diabetes mellitus, excess sugar or insufficient protein in the diet, or from being fed cow's milk	Consult veterinarian. No cure available. Surgical removal of some cataracts is possible.
Insufficient water intake, dehydration, heat, illness, intestinal obstruction (often from wood shavings), parasitism	Determine cause. Increase fluid intake and leafy greens in diet. Clean away anal impacted feces with warm, moist towel. A mineral oil enema may be helpful and if cavy cannot perform coprophagy, supplementation with B vitamins and vitamin K may be necessary. Contact veterinarian immediately. Any decrease in stool production is an emergency. Surgery may be required.
Bacterial or viral infections and diseases, stress, improper diet, hot environment, heatstroke	Consult veterinarian; give fluids; determine cause.
Trauma, injury, poor diet, or genetically inherited	Incisor and molar problems require veterinary care and usually require monthly trimming. Teeth should be trimmed only by a veterinarian.
Bacterial (*Salmonella typhimurium, Salmonella enteritidis, Yersinia pseudo-tuberculosis, Clostridium perfringens, Escherichia coli, Pseudomonas aeruginosa,* or *Listeria monocyto genes*); viral infections (Coronaviruses); parasites (coccidiosis: *Eimeria caviae* and *Cryptosporidium*; worms (usually contracted from grazing on grass contaminated by the feces of other animals); stress or improper diet	Give supportive care, including fluids and force-feeding, if necessary. Isolate from other animals. Consult veterinarian to determine cause.
Infection (*Streptococcus equi, Bordetella bronchiseptica, Streptococcus pneumoniae, Klebsiella, Pasteurella, Actinobacillus*), parasites, injury, disease	Consult veterinarian to determine cause; radiographs (X-rays) may be necessary for a diagnosis.
Infection, injury, irritating substances, disease	Place in a dark area; isolate from other animals; consult veterinarian immediately to prevent loss of vision and/or eye.

Health Problem	Symptoms
Hair loss	Areas of balding or patchy hair
Heatstroke	Hot, weak, unresponsive, comatose
Infections	Symptoms vary depending on the types of germs and severity of the problem
"Lumps"—cervical lymphadenitis	Large abscesses filled with pus in cervical lymph nodes; looks like the mumps; abscesses may recur
Musculoskeletal problems	Pain, lameness, paralysis, stiffness, weight loss, lack of appetite, lethargy
Nails	Torn nail may bleed and become infected
Pododermatitis	Sores and ulcers on the bottom of the feet; pain; inability to walk
Respiratory problems	Wheezing, sneezing, difficulty breathing, discharge from nose and eyes, loss of appetite, inactivity, weight loss
Reproduction problems	Wide variety of reproductive problems, including abortion, dystocia, stillbirths, uterine inertia, uterine hemorrhage, uterine cancer, pregnancy toxemia, eclampsia, cystic ovaries
Skin problems	Loss of hair, sores, flaky or moist skin, redness, oozing, itching, scratching, infection, weight loss
Trauma	Inactivity, lack of appetite, inability to walk or sit normally, broken bones, bleeding, swelling, pain
Urinary tract problems	Weight loss, lack of appetite, lethargy, difficulty urinating, blood in urine, infections, blockages Sows: spots of blood on the floor of cage or on vulva Boars: inability to urinate, urethral blockage

Causes	What to Do
Barbering by cagemates, self-inflicted hair pulling due to boredom, parasites, hormonal imbalance, dietary deficiency, stress	Provide more hideaways or remove dominant animals; give interesting chew toys; treat parasites.
High temperatures, inadequate ventilation	Remove from hot area; submerge body (not head) in cool water; give fluids as soon as conscious. Take to your veterinarian for emergency follow-up care.
Bacteria, viruses, fungi, protozoa	Consult your veterinarian.
Bacteria *Streptococcus zooepidemicus*, sometimes *Streptobacillus moniliformis*	Surgical excision of affected lymph nodes
Deficiencies in vitamin C, vitamin D, or vitamin E; osteoarthritis, diseases, injury	Contact your veterinarian to determine cause and treatment and obtain pain medication.
Injury	Trim nail; give soft bedding, and keep clean.
Wire mesh or abrasive cage floors, heavy animals	Clean, soak, and wrap feet, give soft bedding, consult veterinarian.
Bacterial infection is the most serious (*Bordetella bronchiseptica* and *Streptococcus* pneumoniae); chlamydial infection *Chlamydophila caviae*; or viral infection (adenovirus and paramyxoviruses: Sendai virus, Simian Virus 5, and pneumonia virus of mice). Other causes: allergies, exposure to fine dusts, drafts, or cold, damp environment, lung cancer	Contact your veterinarian immediately before pneumonia develops; isolate from other pets.
Wide variety of causes, including infection, cancer, hormonal imbalances, trauma, and endocrine changes caused by pregnancy	Contact your veterinarian immediately. The majority of these problems are life-threatening and require medications; some require emergency surgery. Many of these problems can be prevented by having your cavy spayed (ovariohysterectomy) or neutered (castration).
Bacterial or fungal infections, parasitism (mites: *Trixacarus, Chirodiscoides*, and others; lice *Gliricola, Gyropus,* and others; fleas; fungi: *Cryptococcus, Trichophyton,* and others), disease, improper diet, stress, unsanitary housing conditions, allergies, hormonal imbalance	Consult veterinarian for diagnosis and medication; keep skin and fur clean.
Many possible types of injuries, such as bite wounds, being dropped, broken bones, hernias from trauma	Observe closely; determine extent of injury; isolate from other pets; contact veterinarian. Some injuries will require surgery.
Stone in the bladder or urethra due to bacterial infection or improper diet; urinary tract infection	Contact your veterinarian immediately. Surgery is necessary to remove stones. Eliminate alfalfa and other hays and greens that are high in calcium and oxalates; discuss value of magnesium hydroxide supplementation with your veterinarian; make sure fresh water is available at all times.

Chapter Nine

Grooming Your Cavy

A healthy cavy will groom itself frequently and do its best to stay clean. You can help your pet stay clean by giving him the right kind of bedding material and changing the bedding frequently to keep the cage clean.

All cavies, even cavies that groom themselves meticulously, need help keeping their hair (cavies have hair, not fur) in top condition. Grooming your pet is an important part of his health care program. It's also fun for both of you. Your cavy will enjoy the stimulating massage from a gentle brush or light combing and you will find grooming your pet is not only a way to show him affection, but it is soothing for you as well. Studies have shown that some people can lower their blood pressure just by caressing or touching a pet.

Of course, your cavy will have to be accustomed to being groomed for the grooming session to be relaxing and enjoyable and you will need a few basic supplies. With just a few minutes of time invested each week, your pet will look like he's ready for the show table, whether he stays at home or competes in exhibits among the fanciest of his kind.

Make It Fun

Grooming should always be a positive experience for your cavy and an enjoyable activity for you. Many cavy owners groom their pets as a form of relaxation and artistic expression. Your pet normally craves close human contact and will love the special attention he receives during the grooming session. While you are brushing your cavy, check him thoroughly for any health problems or skin conditions, such as weight loss, dry or oily skin, hair loss, lumps, bumps, parasites, and scabs.

Just as you will need some practice to become skilled at grooming, especially if you own long-haired cavies, your pet will require a little bit of training to learn to sit quietly on your lap or on a tabletop.

Warning: Never leave your cavy unattended on a table where he could fall and be injured.

All it takes is a few minutes of gentle guidance and training in the beginning. Hold your cavy gently on your lap and speak to him reassuringly as you gently brush him. In the beginning you should limit these "training sessions" to five min-

or standing, and use a nonslip mat on the tabletop.

5. Place a soft brush lightly on your pet's back, then gently brush the surface of the coat. If your little companion has long hair, you may use a comb for more difficult areas after your pet is used to a brush.

6. Cavies bore easily, so limit sessions to three to five minutes, unless your pet is clearly having fun.

7. Several short training sessions are better than one long one.

8. Make sure the table surface is nonslip, to prevent falls or injury.

9. Place all the grooming items you will need to use near the grooming table, within easy reach.

10. Give a small food reward at the conclusion of each grooming session.

Supplies

- Soft boar-bristle brush
- Wire brush with plastic-tipped bristles
- Small comb
- Blunt-tipped scissors (to remove difficult knots or mats)
- Paper wraps for long-haired cavies to protect their hair and keep it clean
- A clean, warm, damp cloth for gently wiping around the eyes and ears
- Disposable tissue for cleaning around the anus when necessary
- Baby fingernail trimmers for the toenails

utes or less, unless you can see that your cavy is thoroughly enjoying the experience. If your pet is unhappy or starting to struggle to get away, stop brushing him and let him rest for a while. You can start again the next day. It won't take long for your cavy to realize that grooming is a pleasant experience.

Here are some tips on how to make grooming a positive experience for your cavy:

1. Begin training for grooming as soon as possible.

2. Be gentle and patient.

3. Speak reassuringly to your pet the entire time.

4. If you prefer to use a table instead of your lap, select a table that is high enough for you to work at a comfortable height, depending on whether you prefer to work sitting

Coat Care

Most short-haired cavies (Americans) require little more than a good weekly brushing and a nail trim when necessary; however, if you have a few minutes each day to tend to coat care, all the better. Excellent results are obtained by stroking the animal with your fingers in the direction of hair growth, to help shed loose hairs and distribute the natural oils through the hair to make it shine.

If you are planning on exhibiting your short-haired cavies, you can bathe them one to three days before the show so they will look their best when it's time to compete.

Cavies with rosettes don't look very good after a bath, so if you have an Abyssinian, don't give him a bath unless he's dirty and really needs one. After a bath the Abyssinian's coat will seem soft and woolly and can take a week or two to return to its normal condition and appearance.

Hair Wraps

Long-haired cavies (Peruvians and Silkies) need a lot of grooming and hair care to look their very best and prevent mats, knots, and tangles. They need to have their hair wrapped, starting at about three to four months of age, when the hair is long enough. The coat may need up to five or six hair wraps and the wraps need to be replaced every two to four days to keep the hair clean.

You can use paper towels, soft cotton cloth, or freezer paper (waxy on one side) as hair wraps. Fold the material in thirds lengthwise and comb the hair and lay it in the center section of the wrap. Fold the outer sides (left and right) over the hair on the center section. Next, take the

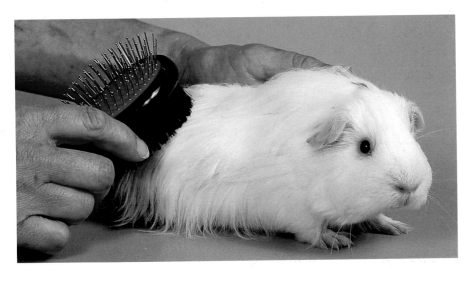

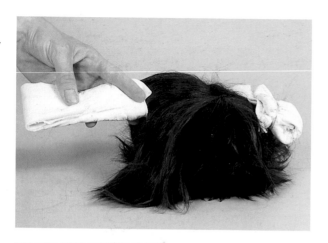

other cavy owners and exhibitors. Many of them have their own secret tricks of the trade that they can share with you. Breeders all have their own methods. As time goes on, you will develop the technique that works best for you to enhance your fancy pet's appearance.

Keep in mind that the perfect coat takes time to develop and is not accomplished overnight. It takes time to grow a great coat, sometimes more than a year.

A beautiful coat is the result of hours and hours of regular grooming. It is a testimony to the excellent care, proper nutrition, clean housing, and love and attention your cavy has received from you.

Teeth and Toenails

While you are grooming your cavy, check his incisor teeth to be sure they are correctly aligned and do not require trimming. Check the teeth at least once a week.

Be sure to check your pet's toenails to be sure they are not overgrown. It is important to keep the nails trimmed so that they do not snag, tear, or bleed. A torn toenail can be painful and become infected. Unless the nail bed has been damaged, the toenail will grow back. In the meantime, the injury should be kept clean to prevent infection.

You can help your cavy keep his nails worn down by giving him a flat

end of the folded wrap and fold it widthwise three or four times and fasten it with a rubber band. Do not fasten it too tightly next to the skin.

Most cavies will object to the wraps and try to chew them out. Be patient and keep up the maintenance. Don't let time go by without grooming your pet and replacing the wraps, because if you do he will lose hair and develop mats and tangles.

If you are planning on exhibiting your long-haired cavies, consult with sandstone to walk on in an area of the cage. But if the nails become too long, you need to take action before they start to grow in different directions and interfere with your pet's movement and hinder his ability to walk comfortably and correctly.

Cutting Toenails

Cutting toenails is something most pet owners dread, but it really isn't difficult. If you handle your cavy's feet from the time he is very young, he will be used to having you touch his feet and restrain them when it's time to cut the toenails.

You can trim the nail carefully using nail clippers designed for human babies. These small clippers work well for tiny cavy nails. Push the hair back from the nail and examine it closely. You will notice each toenail curves and tapers into a point. If the toenail is not too dark in color, you will be able to see pink inside of the toenail, or the "quick."

Natural Way to Help Keep Toenails Trim

Put a flat lava stone in your cavy's play area. Each time your pet walks over the top of it, the tips of the nails will be lightly sanded and gradually the tips will wear smooth. Just be sure the lava stone doesn't take up the entire cage floor space and that your cavy has plenty of soft bedding for his feet.

Ouch!

If you accidentally cut a toenail too closely and you do not have styptic powder available, you may be able to stop the bleeding by pushing the end of the toenail into a soft piece of wax or dipping it in some flour or cornstarch. This will serve as a plug until the bleeding stops.

This is the blood supply and just below it is the excess nail growth that you will remove. When you trim your pet's torn nail, just trim the very tip of it to prevent bleeding and additional damage.

If the toenails are too dark to tell where the quick ends, you can illuminate the nail with a penlight or a flashlight to find the line of demarcation where the blood supply ends. Cut only the very tip of the toenail. If

the nail is still too long, continue to remove the end of the nail carefully in small increments. If you accidentally cut too close, you can stop the bleeding by applying styptic powder (a yellow clotting powder commercially available from your pet store or veterinarian) or by applying pressure with a clean cloth to the toenail for a few minutes.

When the nail trimmer becomes dull it should be replaced so it does not break, shred, or crack the nails. Be sure to praise your cavy for being good and give him a tiny food reward. Without your cavy's cooperation, nail trimming can be very challenging.

Bathtime

Sometimes cavies need to be bathed. For example, if your cavy is very dirty, has a skin condition that requires improved hygiene, has knots or mats that have accumulated dirt and debris, or if he has been ill and has dried feces stuck in his hair, a bath is often the best solution.

When you bathe your pet, make sure that the water is at a comfortable temperature, lukewarm at 77 to 80°F (25 to 27°C). Fill the sink or a plastic pan just a few inches deep.

Gently place your pet in the water and support his body so he doesn't panic or slip. Don't submerge your pet underwater, and take care that his head remains above water and he doesn't inhale water into his lungs. Even though cavies are excellent swimmers, your cavy needs to be supervised at all times while he is in the water. Never leave your cavy alone in the sink or plastic pan!

You can wash your cavy with a gentle, hypoallergenic, emollient, soap-free shampoo available from your veterinarian. Just be sure the shampoo does not contain any harsh chemicals or pesticides—do not use flea and tick

shampoos! A gentle conditioner can help return oils and a natural sheen to your pet's coat. Ask your veterinarian and local cavy club members which shampoo and conditioning products they recommend.

Rinse your pet well, wrap him in a towel, and dry him gently. You can blow-dry the coat with a hair dryer set on warm (not hot) if it doesn't frighten your cavy. Make sure your cavy is completely dry before you put him back in his cage, and don't leave him where there are drafts or where he can become chilled and, thus, more susceptible to pneumonia.

Bright Eyes and Clean Ears

Check your cavy's eyes daily. Make sure pieces of bedding material are not irritating the eyes. Gently remove accumulated dust, dirt, or mucus from the corners of his eyes with a soft, clean, damp tissue.

Wipe from the inside corner of the eye out toward the nose. By checking and cleaning your cavy's eyes, you help prevent them from becoming infected. If your cavy has an eye infection, his eyelids may be reddened, swollen, or crusty. He may have a yellow or green discharge from his eyes. The surface of his eyes may look cloudy, and he may squint if they are painful.

Cavies secrete a whitish fluid from their eyes that is believed to lubricate their eyes. This ocular secretion is normal. Cavies remove the substance with their front paws and spread it through their hair when they wash their faces.

Gently wipe the inside of the ears with a clean, damp cloth or a soft cotton swab. Don't let water go into the ear canals and do not try to stick the cotton swab down the ear canals. If you see excessive dirt in the ears or if they have a bad odor, contact your veterinarian immediately. The condition may be caused by parasites and can be painful.

Chapter Ten

Special Care for Orphan Pups

One day you may find yourself in the unexpected and challenging situation in which you must provide care to one or more baby cavies. This can occur if you buy a young cavy and she is already pregnant, but you are unaware of her condition, and she later has difficulty giving birth or is unable to raise her pups. She may not be able to care for her pups because of complications related to farrowing, or because she is unable to produce milk (agalactica), or because she is not a good mother and will not tend to her young. In any case, the responsibility of taking care of one or more very tiny babies with special dietary needs has now fallen on your shoulders.

Here are some things you can do to help improve the chances of survival for the pups and to make this challenge a little less overwhelming.

Fostering

If the mother of your cavy pups should die or cannot make milk, if you are lucky enough to have other lactating sows in your home, you can convince one of them to adopt the pups. This is called fostering or cross-fostering.

It is best if the foster mother has a small litter of pups the same age as the orphans. Older pups tend to push the younger ones away from the nipples and make it difficult for them to suckle. In extreme cases, the smaller pups could lose weight and possibly starve. If you have more than one sow with a litter, you can split the orphans between two or more dams.

Remove the foster mother and place her in a cage with plenty of food and water. Put the orphans pups in a box with the foster mother's pups, along with bedding material from the adoptive mother's cage. Leave the pups together in the box for 20 minutes. This will help the orphans to smell like the foster mother's own pups and fool her into thinking they are her own.

Return the mother to her cage and carefully introduce the orphans. Stay close by to watch their interactions and behavior. If the mother shows any signs of aggression toward the orphans, remove them immediately and put them back in the box with the foster mother's pups for another 20 minutes and try again. If the mother nudges the orphans away, she is rejecting them. You can keep pushing the pups up next to her and, eventually, she may accept them and allow them to suckle.

If the foster mother continues to reject the pups, smear a little bit of mentholated vapor rub on all of the pups and the chin of the mother. This will mask the differences in odors between her own pups and the orphans, so that she can no longer tell them apart. If all goes well, she will then accept all of the pups in her cage.

After the foster mother accepts the orphans and allows them to suckle, supervise their activities for an hour to be sure all is going well. Don't leave the orphans with the mother until you are certain she will nurse them and take care of them.

It is critical for pups to receive mother's colostrum (a substance that contains important antibodies and nutrients) for their first meal and milk during the first week of life. After one

week of age, pups are easier to hand raise and have a greater chance of survival.

Hand-raising Orphans

If you don't have a foster mother to take over the pups, then you will have to hand-raise the pups yourself. It's not easy to hand-raise orphan cavies, so try not to be too discouraged. Even with lots of patience, hard work and dedication, half of hand-raised cavy pups less than one week of age die. Pups do not eat solids in the first 12 to 24 hours after birth, and day-old orphans frequently die of dehydration.

If you are in the difficult and challenging position of hand-raising newborn pups, be prepared for long, sleepless nights and a small chance of success. However, when the babies survive and thrive, you will feel a true sense of reward and accomplishment—well deserved, indeed!

Cavy pups need to be fed every two to three hours during the day (from 6:00 A.M. through 8 P.M.) and every four to five hours during the night. Tiny newborns can be fed with a tuberculin syringe (without a needle), and week-old pups will lap up their formula directly from a spoon or from a very small jar lid. Watch them closely so you will know exactly how much each pup eats. Keep notes for yourself on their food consumption and weight gain.

Formula for Orphan Cavies Under One Week of Age

- 1/3 ounce (10 g) guinea pig pellets (make sure these contain calcium)
- 1/3 ounce (10 g) rolled oats
- *Tiny* pinch of salt (no more than .5 g)
- 1/30 ounce (1 g) of dextrose (available from your veterinarian). In an emergency you can substitute a *small pinch* of sugar or 15 drops (1 ml) of white grape juice or 15 drops (1 ml) of corn syrup.
- 1/15 ounce (2 g) active dry yeast
- 10 mg vitamin C (available in tablet or liquid form from your pharmacy)
- .5 mg thiamine (available from your veterinarian)
- 3½ ounces (approximately 100 ml) of bottled water

Blend thoroughly and warm formula to body temperature (do not make it hot!).

Use a tuberculin syringe (without a needle) to feed.

Give 5 to 10 drops (.3 ml to .6 ml) every two hours for newborns.

Increase to 10 to 15 drops (.6 to 1 ml) every two to three hours at one week of age, depending on the size of the pup.

Make sure the mixture is prepared fresh daily. Vitamin C will deteriorate.

Your veterinarian can provide you with commercial formulas and make formula recommendations, but in case of emergency, here is a formula to tie you over until you can contact your veterinarian.

Make sure the pups don't go too long between feedings. If they are too hungry, they will try to suckle each other. This can lead to medical problems, including prolapse of the rectum.

Tips for Success

- *Be patient!* It takes a long time for the pups to eat a tiny amount.
- *Do not overfeed! Several small meals are safer than fewer large meals.* If you see formula coming out of the animal's nostrils it means that the liquid has probably gone into the lungs. If this happens, the animal will likely develop pneumonia and die.
- *Do not feed newborn pups cow's milk or products containing cow's milk.*
- *Do not feed chopped vegetables.*

In addition to feeding the orphan pups, you will have to stimulate them to urinate and defecate after meals. They cannot yet eliminate on their own. You can do this by taking a warm, damp, cloth and *lightly dabbing* (do not rub!) their anogenital area.

Keep the pups warm (not hot!) by placing a heating pad, set at *low heat*, under *half* of their housing area. This way, if they get too warm, they can move to the part of their cage where the floor isn't heated. *Do not use a heat lamp to warm the pups. If placed too close it will burn and dehydrate the babies.*

Weaning

A weaned animal is an animal that no longer requires and is not receiving nourishment from its mother's milk. Cavy pups can eat small amounts of solid food within a few days of birth, but they need their mother's milk until they are at least two weeks of age, preferably three.

When you wean the pups, do so gradually. Reduce the number of hand-feedings slightly each day starting at three weeks of age and continue for the next week. Make sure that solid food is available to the pups at all times.

Imprinting

Imprinting is what takes place when a very young animal sees another animal and immediately forms a close bond with it. In the wild, baby animals almost always imprint on their mothers. She is the first thing they see, smell, hear, and recognize. They depend on her for protection. They follow her and learn from her. The same is true for cavies. If the pups' mother died at birth and you are hand-raising them, the pups will imprint on you. They will form a strong bond with you, and the frequent handling they receive will make them very gentle, affectionate pets. The pups will quickly recognize you as a friend and provider of food and look forward to your visits.

Sexing the Pups

It is not hard to tell the sex of the pups at an early age. Hold the pup carefully, belly up, with its back supported against the palm of your hand. Find the anus and look directly above it. If the pup is a male, it will appear to have a slit just above the anus. If the pup is a female, it will have a skin fold in a Y-shape above the anus. The female also has an external urethral opening separate from the vagina.

To identify the sheathed penis, gently palpate, or press around the lower abdomen. With your thumb, use a *gentle*, downward motion along the midline of the lower abdomen. This will cause the penis to protrude from the sheath. It is recognizable by its shape and the two prongs at its tip.

To confirm the sex of the female, retract the vulvar lips and identify the vaginal closure membrane.

The Pups Leave Home

After the pups are weaned, they can be housed like the adults. They have the same needs: nutritious food, fresh water, interesting toys, comfortable temperature, safe, escape-proof housing, companionship, and lots of attention. It's time to find them a new home!

The final stage in raising the orphans is making sure that the youngsters are

going to loving homes where they will receive good care.

To be sure everything goes well for the pups, give the new owners as much information as you can about their care. Show them the type of cage you use to house your cavies. Demonstrate how to pick up the animals and examine them. Give the new owners a bag of the guinea pig food you are currently feeding to prevent the stress of a change in diet. Give the new owners information about the American Cavy Breeders Association. And in case of a problem, recommend any veterinarians you know who have a special interest or expertise in cavies.

After you have successfully handraised the baby cavies, you will surely agree that, in the end, the most difficult thing of all was parting with them!

Chapter Eleven
The Cavy Connoisseur

Every cavy is unique. Each has its own delightful personality, coat color, and type. Many are gifted with beautiful patterns and markings. It seems there's no limit to what a knowledgeable breeder can create. Of course, many pet cavies are born from a mix of different breeds, just like mixed-breed dogs and cats. Mixed breeds are usually sold in pet stores, but for the perfectionist who wants a companion that is classy, elegant, and has a touch of the exotic, purebred cavies are the answer. The best way to find a purebred is to contact a reputable cavy breeder through the American Cavy Breeders Association (ACBA) (see Useful Addresses and Literature).

It takes an eye for beauty, an appreciation of the breeds, an understanding of basic genetics, knowledge of the cavy "Standard of Perfection," and a lot of study and enthusiasm to make the leap from cavy aficionado to cavy connoisseur. Are you ready?

Colors and Breeds

There are currently 13 breeds recognized by the American Cavy Breeders Association. There are also other breeds recognized outside of the United States that may one day be added to the list of breeds accepted for exhibition by the ACBA.

- Abyssinian
- Abyssinian Satin
- American
- American Satin
- Coronet
- Peruvian
- Peruvian Satin
- Silkie
- Silkie Satin
- Teddy
- Teddy Satin
- Texel
- White-crested

The Cavy Kaleidoscope

The genetics of coat color inheritance in the cavy is a *very* complicated subject. To be successful, the breeder must have a firm understanding of basic genetic principles as well as cavy genetics. In the early years following the importation of cavies into Europe and North America, cavy coat color inheritance was studied extensively, although details of genetic inheritance were unclear at that time.

Cavy Varieties

Marked	Base color (usually white) with patterns of a different color on the base color.
Agouti	"Wild-type" coloration, found also in wild cavies. The hair has various bands of color along the shaft (usually shades of buff, golden brown, red, brown, dark brown, black) to give a stippled or peppered appearance to the hair (useful for camouflage in the wild). The overall coat has a "ticked" appearance. Agouti colors include dilute, golden, and silver.
Self	Uniform, unspotted color; no marking and no pattern. Colors include beige, black, chocolate, cream, lilac, red, red-eyed orange, and white.
Solid	Uniform or mixed color; no marking; no pattern. Colors include brindle, dilute solid, golden solid, roan, and silver solid.

In the early 1900s, Sewall Wright and W. E. Castle began to study cavy coat color genetics in depth. Their work spanned more than 50 years and Wright published many scientific papers on the topic. A brief summary of Wright's work is explained in Searle's book (see Useful Addresses and Literature).

Today's scientists have turned their attention from color genetics to topics of pressing medical interest. This leaves the continuing challenge of figuring out coat type and color

inheritance right in the hands of cavy fanciers. For the dedicated, educated cavy breeder, there are still more cavy genetic mysteries waiting to be solved.

The American Cavy Breeders Association currently recognizes 22 varieties of colors or color patterns. As breeders continue to learn more about genetics and experiment with their breeding programs, it is certain more breeds and varieties will be created and possibly accepted by the ACBA.

Cavy Colors

- Beige—beige with pink eyes.
- Black—deep, dark black with black eyes.
- Brindle—a mixture or blend of red and black hairs with dark eyes.
- Broken—a coat with patches of two or more colors.
- Chocolate—a deep, rich, chocolate brown color with brown eyes.
- Cream—off-white color with dark or red eyes.

- Dalmatian—white with dark spots well distributed throughout the coat, black head with broad white blaze, black ears and feet, and ruby or dark eyes.
- Dutch—white "saddle" around the back and under the belly; dark facial markings with a white blaze down the center of the face, dark chest, neck, and front legs.
- Golden agouti—chestnut with blue-black undercoat, golden with dark ticking, and dark eyes.
- Himalayan—white with smudge of chocolate, dark brown, or black on the nose, ears and feet match color on nose. Eyes are pink. Himalayans are born white and may be mistaken for self whites. They do not develop their full markings and complete col-

oration until they are six months of age or more.
- Lilac—purple-gray coat and eyes that are pink or dark with a red hue.
- Red—deep red with dark eyes.
- Red-eyed orange—reddish orange coat and ruby eyes.
- Roan—white hairs mingled with one or two darker colors, such as red and black. Eyes are dark.
- Silver agouti—silvery white with blue-black undercoat and dark eyes.
- Tortoiseshell—well-defined patches of red and black evenly distributed throughout the body, should look much like a checkerboard. Eyes are dark.
- Tortoiseshell and white—alternating patches of red, black, and white on each side of the body. There is

a dividing line down the middle of the back and the middle of the belly. Eyes are dark.

- White—clean, pure white color with no discoloration and no yellow tinge. Eyes are dark.

Recognized Breeds

Sensational Satins

Several of the recognized breeds also come in a Satin version. Satins differ from their non-Satin counterparts by the beautiful natural sheen that makes their hair glisten. The sheen is due to a recessive gene that causes the hollow hair shafts to reflect light. Satins have finer hair than their counterparts. The iridescent gloss is most noticeable in smooth-coated, short-haired breeds, although it adds a beautiful luster to long-coated breeds. Satins are considered as separate breeds.

Abyssinian and Abyssinian Satin

As you already know, the cavy is no stranger to misnomers. So it should come as no surprise that the word Abyssinian, as exotic as it sounds, has nothing to do with the origin of this wonderful variation in coat type. Inappropriately named, but admired just the same, the Abyssinian drew much attention and admiration from cavy fanciers in England in the 1800s. More than a century later, the Abyssinian remains extremely popular worldwide.

The Abyssinian is easy to identify. It is embellished with deep, full, round, tall rosettes all over its body. (Rosettes are whorls of harsh hair that radiate evenly from a pinpoint center giving the animal a tufted appearance.) But these are not random rosettes. There should be at least eight, and ideally ten. The

rosettes should be arranged as set forth in the Abysinnian "Standard of Perfection," so that the animal has a checkerboard appearance. Rosettes can be seen on pups as young as two days of age.

Abysinnians come in a wide variety of colors including self, solid, agouti, marked, red, roan, brindle, and tortoiseshell and white. Armed with rosettes and intense color, a quality Abysinnian or Abysinnian Satin is hard to beat.

American and American Satin

The American is a smooth, short-haired breed with a rounded, Roman nose, rose petal-shaped ears, and a rounded body that is the same width from the shoulders down to the hips. It is arguably the most popular cavy in the United States and reported to be the calmest of the cavy breeds.

The American was the first type of cavy imported from South America into Europe and North America and has retained its popularity throughout the centuries.

American Satins were the first Satins recognized by the ACBA. They reportedly appeared in a herd in 1976 and became a breed all their own in 1984. They resemble the Americans except for their Satin coats. The Satin sheen can be seen on newborn pups, then it tends to go away until the animal is about three months of age. The luster is striking by four months of age.

American cavies come in a wide variety including beige, black, chocolate, cream, red, red-eyed orange, white roan golden, silver, dilute agouti, golden agouti, silver agouti, broken, Dalmatian, Himalayan, and tortoiseshell and white.

Peruvian and Peruvian Satin

The Peruvian is a silky, long-haired cavy that first appeared in Paris in the late 1800s. It received its name from T. L. Sclater of the Zoological Society of London and is the ancestor of our modern-day long-haired breeds.

Peruvians have the longest hair of all the cavy breeds. Long facial hair falls forward over the eyes, making it difficult for the untrained eye to know which end is the front and which is the rear. Long hair parts down the middle of the back and is dense, soft, and silky with two rosettes on the rump. Peruvians *must* have rosettes, and in addition to those on the rump, low saddle rosettes are permissible. (They should not have rosettes on the back of the neck or up high on the back.)

Peruvians are known for their lively personality and are considered by many to be the second most popular cavy breed. They require a lot of grooming to keep their soft, flowing hair free of knots and mats and looking their best.

Peruvians and Silkies were referred to as Angoras in earlier times but are now called by their respective breed names.

Peruvians come in several varieties including black, cream, red, white, broken, and tortoiseshell and white.

Silkie and Silkie Satin (Sheltie)

The Silkie has very long, dense hair that grows rapidly, almost 1 inch (2.2 cm) every month. It has short facial hair, especially around its broad, blunt, Roman nose, and a long mane that sweeps backward and blends in with the hairs of the rump, without parting. Silkies do not have rosettes.

The Silkie was first observed in Peruvian litters in the early 1930s but it wasn't until 1980 that it gained acceptance as a separate breed in the United States, and the Silkie Satin was officially recognized in 1987. (The Silkie was recognized as a separate breed in the United Kingdom in 1973, where it is referred to as a Sheltie.)

Silkies are available in solid, self, agouti, marked, broken, tortoiseshell and white, white, and Himalayan.

White-crested

The White-crested cavy looks like the ideal smooth-coated American with a single *white* rosette placed precisely and neatly in the middle of its forehead. Very cute! But be forewarned—the perfect White-crested cavy is difficult to obtain. It should not have white anywhere else on its body except its crest. White-crested cavies come in different colors. You can decide for yourself whether red, red-eyed orange, black, lilac, cream, or brindle look best with a white crest.

The White-crested cavy was the fourth cavy breed recognized by the ACBA. Accepted by the ACBA in 1974, it was recently ranked as the fifth most popular cavy breed.

Coronet

When cavy breeders bred Crested cavies with Silkie cavies, the result was the irresistibly charming Coronet. The Coronet was recognized as a breed in the United States in 1997.

This wonderful animal has the best of both worlds: the beautiful flowing coat of a Silkie, plus the decorative crest, or crown, of the Crested cavy. The crest grows very long and eventually falls over or covers the eyes. It's important to check under the hair regularly to be sure the eyes are bright and clear.

Teddy and Teddy Satin

The Teddy looks like a fuzzy, kinky, frizzy American cavy. Its hair is medium length and easy to groom. The gene for the Teddy's curly hair is autosomal recessive. This means that although some animals may not have Teddy hair, they can be carriers of the gene and able to produce Teddy offspring. The only way to be guaranteed you will have Teddy pups in the litter is to breed a Teddy boar to a Teddy sow.

Some people incorrectly call the Teddy a Rex. The British Rex is not the same as a Teddy. They are two separate breeds with a different genetic makeup.

Teddys are available in a wide variety of colors and patterns including black, cream, red, white, roan, brindle, broken, and tortoiseshell and white.

Teddys are very popular. Their cuddly appearance matches their good nature. They are as sweet and gentle as they look.

Texel

In the short time since it was developed in 1980 (by an English fancier breeding a Silkie to a British Rex), the Texel has become the third most popular cavy breed. It requires a lot of grooming time and, to a certain extent, grooming skill and artistry. It has silky, long ringlets that must be groomed and arranged by hand (a brush or comb will stretch out and ruin the ringlets). The Texel comes in a variety of colors.

Texels are calm, quiet, easy-going animals with sweet dispositions. It's no wonder they are so popular.

Other Breeds

Every breed has its beginnings somewhere, sometime. It starts out as an experimental breeding, or cross between breeds, or an interesting mutation that gives attractive results. If the genetic inheritance can be identified and similar, repeated breedings give consistent results, a "type" eventually is set that becomes separate and is different from the others. In time, the type evolves to such a degree that it merits consideration as a recognizable breed.

Cavy fanciers throughout the world have developed different strains, lines, and varieties of cavies. Some of these are accepted breeds or colors in other countries and some are not yet recognized by the ACBA, although they may be one day in the future.

English

The English cavy has short, smooth, straight hair less than 2 inches (3.8 cm) in length. Most inbred and outbred strains of cavies used in research laboratories are of the English variety. Fortunately, English cavies are extremely popular and the majority of them are kept as pets in loving homes.

English-crested

This breed is recognized in the United Kingdom. It is an English cavy that has a rosette in the center of its forehead, just like the American White-crested cavy. The main difference is that the rosette is not white, but the same color (also called self-crested) as the rest of the animal's body.

Merino

The Merino is a crested Texel with hair that is longer on the rear than the rest of the body.

Alpaca

The Alpaca, or Merino Peruvian, as it is called in Australia, was created by crossing Peruvians with Texels. The result resembles a curly-haired Peruvian with a dense coat and coarse facial hair.

Boucle

Boucle is French for "curl" and the word says it all. This cavy is another version of the Peruvian-Texel cross, this time producing hanging ringlets all over the animal's body.

Lunkarya

This recent variety is still in its "developmental phase." Breeders in Scandinavia are working on perfecting its beautiful curly coat. It is a combination of Peruvian and Teddy genetics.

Skinny Pig

Skinnies are hairless cavies. They can have a few short hairs on their body, especially around the nose, but for the most part they are pretty naked.

Finding the Right Breed

You would think that it would be easy to find exactly what you want for exhibition when you want it, but the truth is many of these variations are inherited in a recessive manner and are not produced often or in large numbers. It may take quite

a while before a breeder can offer you a cavy that comes close to your specifications. You may have to settle for something slightly different than what you had planned on, or be very, very patient until just the right cavy comes along.

Be sure to buy the best cavy you can from an established, reputable breeder who is willing to part with quality animals. There's a lot to learn to be successful at this challenging hobby and you will be starting from scratch. You will need the help and guidance of experienced breeders as you begin your hobby and continue throughout the years.

Here are some things you can do to maximize your chances of success.
• Make sure you have the time, space, and money for your hobby before you begin.

• Start with the best animal stock you can afford.
• Give your animals the best food and housing possible.
• Find an experienced breeder to be your mentor.
• Continue to learn as much as you can about cavies.
• Be patient.
• Keep accurate health records.
• Join your local and national cavy clubs and be an active participant.
• And most of all, have fun!

Identification

If you want to exhibit your cavy, the American Cavy Breeders Association requires safe, permanent identification in the animal's left ear. This can be either an ear tag or a tattoo.

Other forms of identification are not accepted by the ACBA at this time.

1. Ear tags: Ear tags are the preferred method of cavy identification. Use only ear tags approved by the ACBA. These are self-piercing tags size 1 or size 3, available from the National Band and Tag Company (see Information) or a cavy and rabbit equipment supplier. The tags and pliers come with a set of instructions. The tag goes in the left ear.

Make sure the ear is large enough to be tagged so that it doesn't tear out of the ear. Ask your veterinarian or an experienced cavy breeder to help you.

2. Ear tattoos: Ear tattoos require special pliers and ink (usually green ink for pigmented ears and black ink for white ears) and needles. It is a permanent and visible form of identification. Tattoos are applied to the left ear. An experienced cavy breeder can help you with the tattoo.

If you are not exhibiting your cavy, and are not interested in ear tags and tattoos, you might consider asking your veterinarian about a microchip. Microchips are inserted under the skin using a syringe. If your cavy gets lost and someone finds him, a scanner (used by veterinarians and animal shelters) can read his microchip and the information can then be relayed to the microchip registry so that you can be reunited with your little, lost friend.

Crazy About Cavies

With the wide range of cavy breeds and varieties, it's hard to pick a favorite. Like so many other cavy lovers, you may feel the temptation to start an entire collection. You may wonder if you're becoming crazy about cavies. After all, it's not unusual to hear cavy fanciers exclaim, "You can never have too many!" Of course, everything has its limits, but it's fun to dream.

The cavy has proven itself to be the quintessential companion. Calm, quiet, attractive, and loveable, it is often used for pet-facilitated therapy, bringing happiness to senior citizens in nursing homes or cheering up hospitalized children. Cavies have served as excellent educational projects for students active in organizations such as 4-H. They have provided countless hours of enjoyment to fanciers and exhibitors, in the backyard and on the show table. They make ideal pets for people of all ages.

From sacrificial offering to the gods, to culinary delicacy, to research laboratory animal, to nursing homes, to the show table—and into your cozy home—the cavy is a world traveler *and* a time traveler. It has come a long way from the dirt floors of the Peruvian huts its ancestors once scampered thousands of years ago. Some of the mysteries of its fascinating history have been solved, yet so many secrets remain. The cavy is a charming enigma that has benefited humankind in countless ways throughout history. It deserves its status today as an adored pet worldwide.

So, the next time you sit down to snuggle with your cavy and look into his bright eyes and you find yourself crazy about cavies, don't worry. For thousands of years, thousands of people on this planet have felt the same way you do. You're in good company!

Useful Addresses and Literature

Organizations

American Cavy Breeders
　Association
ACBA Secretary
2719 Coventry Lane
Ocoee, FL 34761
www.acbaonline.com

American Rabbit Breeders
　Association
P.O. Box 5667
Bloomington, IL 61702
(309) 664-7500
(309) 664-0941 (Fax)
www.arba.net

American Association of
· Zoo Veterinarians
581705 White Oak Road
Yulee, FL 32097
(904) 225-3275
www.aazv.org

American Veterinary Medical
　Association
1931 North Meacham Road
Suite 100
Schaumberg, IL 60173-4360
(800) 248-2862
www.avma.org

Association of Exotic Mammal
　Veterinarians
618 Church Street, Suite 220
Nashville, TN 37219
www.aemv.org

National Band and Tag Company
751 York Street
P.O. Box 72430
Newport, KY 41072-0430
(859) 261-2035
(800) 261-8247 (Fax)
tags@nationalband.com (E-mail)
www.nationalband.com

Books

Hillyer, E. V., and K. E. Quesenberry. *Ferrets, Rabbits, and Rodents*. Philadelphia: W. B. Saunders Company, 2012.

Laber-Laird, K., M. M. Swindle, and P. Flecknell. *Handbook of Rodent and Rabbit Medicine*. New York: Elsevier Science, 1996.

Lavocat, R. "What Is a hystricomorph?" *The Biology of Hystricomorph Rodents, The Proceedings of a Symposium Held at the Zoological Society of London*, number 34: 7–20. I. W. Rowlands and B. J. Weir, Editors. London: Academic Press, 1974.

Nowak, R. M., Editor. *Walker's Mammals of the World*, 6th edition, Volume II. Baltimore, MD: The Johns Hopkins University Press, 1999.

Searle, A. G. *Comparative Genetics of Coat Colour in Mammals*. London, UK: Logos Press Limited, 1967.

Suckow, M. A., K. A. Stevens, and R. P. Wilson. *The Laboratory Rabbit, Guinea Pig, Hamster, and Other Rodents*. San Diego: Elsevier, 2012.

Wagner, J. E., and P. J. Manning. *The Biology of the Guinea Pig*. New York: Academic Press, 1976.

Wright, S. "Color Inheritance in Mammals—V. The Guinea Pig." *J. Hered.* 8:476–80. 1917.

Important Note

This pet handbook tells the reader how to buy and care for guinea pigs. The advice given in the book applies to healthy animals with good dispositions obtained from a reputable source. Extraordinary efforts have been made by the author and the publisher to insure that treatment recommendations are precise and in agreement with standards accepted at the time of publication. If your guinea pig exhibits any signs of illness you should consult a veterinarian immediately—some diseases are dangerous for human beings. If you have any questions about an illness, or if you have been scratched or bitten by your guinea pig, consult a physician immediately. Some people are allergic to animal hair, dander, saliva, urine, and feces; are immune-suppressed; or are immunologically compromised, and cannot be exposed to animals. If you are not sure, consult your physician before you acquire a guinea pig.

Be sure to instruct children in the safe handling of guinea pigs and supervise children when they are handling guinea pigs. Never leave your pets or small children alone with guinea pigs.

If your guinea pig escapes, to prevent electrical accidents, be sure that it cannot gnaw on electrical wires and remember your guinea pig may cause you to fall if it runs between your feet and you are trying not to step on it.

The author and publisher assume no responsibility for and make no warranty with respect to results that may be obtained from procedures cited. Neither the author nor the publisher shall be liable for any damage resulting from reliance on any information contained herein, whether with respect to procedures, or by reason of any misstatement, error, or omission, negligent or otherwise, contained in this work. Information contained herein is presented as a reference only and is not a substitution for consultation with veterinarians or physicians.

Index